Business Fumbles!

Learning from Entrepreneurial Mistakes

Sheila Williams, EA

Table of Contents

Chapter 1
Introduction

Entrepreneurship mirrors life in many ways, it's filled with twists, setbacks, growth, and, most importantly, invaluable lessons. Success is rarely achieved in a straight line. More often, it's a winding path where each challenge reveals new insight. Much like a child who matures through experience, entrepreneurs evolve with every mistake and every hard-earned victory. These experiences shape our business identities and set us apart in a crowded landscape.

The business world is in constant motion. Every decision, whether a win or a misstep, teaches us something. However, success isn't just about learning from past failures; it also demands the foresight to anticipate them. This book is a journey through the realities of running a business, revealing the strategies that seasoned entrepreneurs use to thrive and exploring the truths often left out of traditional business education.

Each chapter is a blend of practical knowledge and real-life stories that reflect the day-to-day challenges entrepreneurs face. From understanding market shifts to embracing innovation, this book is designed to be an honest, empowering guide to help you navigate the unpredictable terrain of entrepreneurship.

This project holds profound personal meaning for me. Over the course of my 35+ years in the accounting profession, I've seen countless businesses succeed and fail. Time and time again, I've found that failure isn't always due to a lack of passion or effort; it's often the result of not knowing what you don't know. One story has stayed with me throughout my career. I mentioned this story in my last book, but I feel that it really needs to be a part of this book because it's part of the reason I continue to look for ways to help future business owners.

While working at a CPA firm, I was assigned the financials of a woman who had operated a dance studio for over 25 years. As I reviewed her records, it became clear that she had unknowingly mismanaged her finances for years. During our first meeting, tears streamed down her face as she said, "You've been managing my books for over 15 years, and no one has ever asked me the questions you did. No one ever explained anything to me like this. And now, because I didn't know, I must shut down." That moment was deeply impactful. It made me realize how often business owners carry heavy burdens in silence, and how a lack of knowledge can dismantle even the most passionate dream.

This book was born from those moments, from stories like hers, and from the desire to ensure other entrepreneurs don't face the same fate. Running a business can feel like navigating a dark room without light. With this book, I hope to be the flashlight that illuminates the way, offering practical tools, honest advice, and a sense of direction.

Today, starting a business can feel overwhelming. A quick internet search reveals a flood of information, some useful, much of it contradictory or confusing. There's advice on creating business plans, forming LLCs, obtaining licenses, understanding taxes, and more. But what's missing is real-world, experience-based guidance that helps entrepreneurs navigate the gray areas. This book is here to bridge that gap.

Let me be clear: I don't claim to have all the answers. Despite my decades in accounting and entrepreneurship, I continue to learn every single day. What I do offer are lived experiences, hard lessons, and insight drawn from working closely with a wide range of business owners, many of whom had exceptional ideas, strong customer service, and boundless drive, but still didn't make it.

Ask yourself this: Have you ever loved a small business, admired their passion, appreciated their service, and then, one day, noticed they were gone? You wonder what went wrong. Was it poor financial planning? Personal spending disguised as business expenses? A bad partnership? Burnout? In this book, we'll explore the most common reasons businesses fail and how you can avoid those same traps.

My own entrepreneurial journey wasn't without its missteps. Despite having a strong accounting background, I wasn't prepared for the challenges of managing people, leading a team, balancing operations, and building systems that didn't rely entirely on me. I fell into the trap of micromanagement, thinking no one could do things the way I could. But over time, I realized that with clear direction and proper training, my team could thrive, and so could I.

I started with no roadmap. No blueprint. No instruction manual. Like many others, I stumbled, fell, and got back up again. Eventually, I understood that business success goes beyond numbers. It requires leadership, emotional intelligence, adaptability, and the willingness to let go of control.

Even after reaching the 10-year mark in my business, I still find myself learning and correcting mistakes. I continue to see businesses around me closing their doors, and I can't help but ask: Is there something successful business owners know that others don't? Is there a secret formula they're not sharing?

To find answers, I launched my podcast, Business Fumbles. I invited fellow business owners, some wildly successful, others still finding their way, to share their stories. What I discovered was enlightening. Many of them faced the same challenges I did. Some had stumbled in the exact same way. What I learned was this: there is no secret recipe. No magic formula. Just commitment, consistency, humility, and the courage to keep showing up.

That realization is what inspired this second book. While my first book opened the conversation, this one goes deeper. Business Fumbles is my open letter to entrepreneurs, to those who are in the trenches and to those just getting started. It's a raw, honest exploration of what it truly takes to build and sustain a business.

My hope is that within these pages, you'll find more than just advice. You'll find real stories, practical strategies, and a sense of solidarity. I want to equip you with the tools to build a strong foundation, avoid common pitfalls, recover from setbacks, and ultimately thrive.

So, welcome. Let's walk this road together, through mistakes, through growth, and toward a more sustainable, fulfilling vision of success.

Chapter Two
A Recipe for Reality

Jon grew up in a lively African American household with four kids, two parents, and a backyard that always smelled like smoked ribs and family. Weekends weren't just "days off." They were events. The kind where everyone pulled up with lawn chairs, aunties argued about who made the best potato salad, and kids ran through sprinklers while grown folks laughed over games of spades.

The real star of those gatherings, though, was the grill.

Jon's father treated barbecue like a sacred ritual. He washed the ribs, trimmed the excess fat, seasoned them with confident hands, then slapped the meat like it was misbehaving, followed by a wink to Jon's mom.

"This batch right here? Oh, it's going to be good."

That confidence stuck with Jon. It wasn't just about the food. It was the feeling. Happiness. The way people gathered around something he created.

As Jon grew up, he inherited the grill like a crown. At every family event, he was behind the smoke. His wife would stand nearby, admiring him like he was a celebrity chef.

"Baby," she'd say, smiling, "you cook so good. We should open a restaurant."

One day, those words became reality.

The Dream Begins

Jon began selling plates from home. Word spread fast, first through family, then co-workers, then complete strangers knocking on the door asking,

"Y'all still got plates left?"

The food was amazing, but financially, nothing added up. Jon noticed that after every grocery run, they seemed to be spending more than they were making.

"We just need more customers," he thought.

So they promoted harder with flyers, Facebook posts, and specials. And it worked. Orders increased, and eventually the community convinced them to take the next leap.

They opened a small restaurant.

The grand opening was everything Jon dreamed of. Lines out the door. Compliments flying. Customers posting pictures online with captions like, "Best BBQ in the city!"

Money was coming in. Smiles were everywhere.

Life felt good. Except they were running blind.

The Problem They Never Saw Coming

There was no bookkeeping system.

No QuickBooks. No accountant.

Their financial method was simple:

"If the bank account has money, we're doing good."

Every receipt, invoice, and expense went into a shoebox. At the end of the year, they handed everything to a tax preparer and assumed that was enough.

Then came the letter from the State Department of Taxation.

PAST DUE SALES TAXES

Two years. Jon was confused.

"We charged sales tax. We collected it. How do we owe anything?"

Because no one ever told him something crucial:

Sales tax collected is never your money.

You are holding it on behalf of the state, and you must file reports and remit that money regularly.

They had collected the sales tax and spent it.

Penalties. Interest. Late fees.

Thousands of dollars owed.

They entered a payment plan and thought they were safe.

Until the air conditioning broke.

Reality Hits Hard

Jon called the landlord, confident the AC would be repaired.

Instead, the landlord sent him a copy of the lease with one line highlighted:

“Tenant is responsible for all maintenance and repairs.”

The repair cost was $2,500. They did not have $2,500.

Customers were sweating. Orders slowed down.

They borrowed the money to fix the AC.

Before they could catch their breath, the landlord delivered another surprise.

“Rent is doubling effective next month.”

No negotiation. No sympathy. Jon looked at his wife.

“What do we do now?”

They pivoted again, this time into a food truck. Lower rent. More mobility. Fewer headaches.

Or so they thought.

The Ugly Side of Hope

The food truck came with its own list of expenses:

- Fuel
- Truck repairs
- Parking fees
- Commissary kitchen rental
- County permits
- New insurance coverage

Every week brought new costs. They were working harder but earning less.

People still loved the food.

But Jon started to realize something devastating.

They weren't running a business.

They were running themselves into the ground.

And finally, Jon faced the truth he never wanted to admit:

Passion got them here.

But a lack of planning was taking them out.

Business Lessons Hidden in Jon's Story

Jon's story is fictional, but its lessons are real. This is what happens when passion launches a business without a plan to sustain it.

① Passion Without Numbers Is Just a Hobby

Jon watched the bank balance instead of tracking profits.

When the account dropped, panic followed.

Business Rule:

Numbers tell the truth. Feelings do not.

Action Step:

Use bookkeeping software or hire a bookkeeper from day one.

② Sales Tax Money Is Not Your Money

Jon collected sales tax and spent it as income. The state demanded it back with penalties.

Business Rule:

Sales tax is a liability held for the state.

Action Step:

Register with your state tax department and file monthly or quarterly.

③ Read Every Lease, Especially the Fine Print

Jon assumed the landlord paid for major repairs.

Business Rule:

Commercial leases protect landlords, not tenants.

Action Step:

Have a real estate attorney review your lease before signing.

④ No Emergency Fund Means Constant Crisis

The AC broke. Rent increased. They had no reserves.

Business Rule:

Every business needs a rainy-day fund.

Action Step:

Save at least two to three months of operating expenses.

⑤ A Pivot Without a Plan Is Just Running Away

The food truck seemed cheaper until hidden costs appeared.

Business Rule:

A new model is not automatically better.

Action Step:

Build a six-month budget before pivoting.

⑥ Busy Doesn't Mean Profitable

Long lines looked like success, but expenses were crushing the business.

Business Rule:

Revenue is vanity. Profit is reality.

Action Step:

Track:

- Cost of goods sold (COGS)
- Labor
- Overhead
- Net profit

Final Thought

Jon's story is not a failure. It is a wake-up call.

Entrepreneurs don't fail because they lack passion.

They fail because they lack preparation.

Before you invest in equipment, decor, or a grand opening, invest in knowledge.

Passion lights the fire. Planning keeps it burning.

The Chef with a Dream and a Lease That Wouldn't Let Go

Tom loved to cook. He wasn't just passionate; he was gifted. From French sauces to handmade Italian pastas, his dishes were crafted with care and skill. He worked a full-time job during the day, but cooking was his escape and his dream.

One day, he shared that dream with a coworker who said excitedly, "I know someone selling their restaurant. I can introduce you."

Within days, Tom was seated with the owner and the landlord. The deal required no upfront purchase price, only a lease transfer. The landlord drafted a new lease with Tom as the primary tenant, and suddenly, Tom had a restaurant.

Tom and his wife invested their savings into paint, decor, signage, and small upgrades.

Opening day was beautiful. Friends and family came out to support him.

Then reality arrived.

The restaurant was in a low-traffic area. After the opening weekend, foot traffic slowed. Delivery apps gained little traction.

Tom adjusted. He changed hours, distributed lunchtime flyers to nearby businesses, and slowly built a customer base.

Encouraged, he took out a business loan for advertising and improvements. Event inquiries came in, but clients required a liquor license and private buyouts. Tom had neither the license nor the ability to close for private events.

He added patio seating to increase capacity, but the climate made outdoor dining impractical.

Then equipment failures hit the business. First, the AC failed. Next, the refrigeration units followed. With no reserves, Tom borrowed more to cover repairs.

By the second year, he was exhausted. Working seven days a week led to burnout. He shortened business hours to recover, but staff income declined, turnover increased, and training drained time and resources.

He explored expansion but discovered his lease locked him in for ten years with guaranteed annual rent increases. Investors walked away. The landlord refused negotiations.

Tom was stuck.

Years passed as he barely stayed afloat. The liquor license remained unattainable due to cost and legal complexity.

The joy faded.

Business Lessons from Tom's Journey

Tom had talent, passion, and product. But planning failures became burdens.

1. Never Sign a Lease Without Legal Review

Solution:

Use an attorney and negotiate exit strategies.

2. Location Matters More Than Aesthetics

Solution:

Analyze foot traffic, parking, and visibility before signing.

3. Word-of-Mouth Isn't Enough

Solution:

Invest early in marketing and community outreach.

4. Loans Should Grow, Not Rescue

Solution:

Maintain emergency funds and forecast monthly expenses.

5. Licensing Must Be Planned in Advance

Solution:

Explore alcohol licensing requirements before opening.

6. Understand Staffing Before Changing Hours

Solution:

Communicate changes early and maintain balanced scheduling.

7. Growth Requires Long-Term Planning

Solution:

Prepare growth strategies at least 12 to 18 months ahead.

Closing Thoughts: When Passion Meets Planning

Jon and Tom's stories may be fictional, but their struggles are real.

Passion sparks the vision. Planning builds the foundation.

Strategy makes the difference between surviving and thriving.

So don't just be inspired. Be prepared.

If these stories resonate with you, tune into the Business Fumbles podcast, where real entrepreneurs share their real journeys, failures, successes, and lessons so you can avoid your next fumble.

Chapter Three
Trust, Trauma, and the Cost of Not Knowing

Lee was one of those women who lit up a room without even trying. Kind-hearted, focused, and driven, she had the kind of spirit that made people believe she was destined for success. Her family migrated to the United States when she was young, chasing opportunity with nothing but determination and the clothes they carried across borders.

Her parents wasted no time building a legacy. They opened a small restaurant, humble but full of heart. Lee started working there before she even understood what "business" meant. She wasn't paid wages. She didn't clock in or out. She helped because that's what family did. She chopped vegetables after school, wiped down tables on weekends, and watched her parents stretch every dollar just to survive.

But while she worked for her family's dream, Lee quietly built one of her own.

She took beauty classes whenever she could, juggling school, restaurant shifts, and studying late into the night. Eventually, she earned her professional license. Every tip, every extra dollar she made doing hair or makeup, she saved. She didn't splurge, didn't brag, didn't tell anyone her plans. She was building safety. She was building freedom.

And by the time she was ready to open her own business, she had enough saved to support herself for over a year.

When Love Turns Into a Business Partner

At a friend's event one evening, she met him, the man she thought was her forever.

He saw her ambition and loved it. She saw his confidence and trusted it.

They fell hard. They married fast. And with her savings and his encouragement, they opened her first salon together. The business grew quickly. Clients adored her, money flowed in, and the couple expanded into more ventures. Then came children, a beautiful home, vacations, nice cars, the life she had dreamed of living.

But somewhere along the line, her husband changed.

He became distant. Quiet. Controlling in ways she couldn't explain but could feel.

Whenever Lee asked about the finances, he brushed her off:

"I got it."

"Don't worry about that."

"You just focus on the customers."

She trusted him.

But trust can be the quickest path to betrayal.

The Discovery That Broke Everything

When divorce proceedings began, the truth came out like a storm she never saw coming.

He had been draining money from the businesses. He had opened accounts she didn't know existed.

He built a business overseas with their money.

He funneled funds to relatives.

He had positioned himself as the "financial head," while she ran everything else.

Lee wasn't just heartbroken. She was blindsided.

The houses, the cars, the land, everything she thought they built together, was now tangled in court battles. She was dividing wealth she created with her own hands and didn't even know had disappeared.

Depression hit hard. She questioned herself every day:

"How did I miss this?"

"Why didn't I protect myself?"

"How could someone I love do this to me?"

But her family refused to let her drown.

Her mother pulled her out of bed and pushed her toward her future.

"Get up. You worked too hard to let someone take your life from you."

With their support, Lee hired a professional accountant who combed through three years of financial records. Those records told the story she never saw: transfers, withdrawals, unexplained payments, and business activity her husband hid from her.

Those documents became evidence.

And slowly, painfully, Lee began reclaiming her power.

She realized something vital:

- She was the business.
- Her name built it.
- Her talent sustained it.
- Her clients came for her, not him.

And while her story is fictional here, it represents real women I've met far too many times, women who trusted blindly, signed nothing, controlled nothing, and lost everything.

Business Lessons from Lee's Journey

(As Told Through the Story Behind the Pain)

Instead of listing rules, let's look at Lee's lessons the way they unfolded in her life, through moments, choices, and realizations that every entrepreneur can learn from.

1. Building a Business Without Paperwork Is Building on Sand

Lee assumed marriage replaced documentation.

Her husband assumed "control" replaced partnership.

Without a partnership agreement, she had no clear claim to the businesses she helped build.

Simple Truth:

When emotions enter business, paperwork must enter first.

Clear ownership percentages.

Defined roles.

Written rights.

Written responsibilities.

Love doesn't replace contracts, ever.

2. The Person Running the Business Should Never Be in the Dark

Lee handled operations, marketing, customer service, clients, and daily work.

Her husband handled the money.

That imbalance created the perfect environment for deception.

Simple Truth:

If your hands build the business, your eyes must see the money.

You need access to:

- Bank accounts
- Processing platforms
- Accounting software
- Tax filings
- Financial statements
- Trust should never remove your access.

3. Mixing Personal and Business Money Is How Problems Hide

- Their accounts blended.

- Their payments blended.
- Expenses and transfers blurred.
- That blur allowed money to disappear.

Simple Truth:

- Boundaries protect your bank account and your sanity.
- Separate accounts.
- Separate credit cards.
- Separate recordkeeping.
- Clean lines create clear truth.

4. An Accountant Isn't a Luxury, It's Protection

When everything fell apart, the accountant wasn't just doing a job.

She became the light that exposed the truth.

Simple Truth:

A third party sees what love makes you overlook.

Quarterly reviews.

Annual audits.

Monthly bookkeeping.

These aren't chores, they're shields.

5. Don't Let Love Silence Your Logic

Lee ignored red flags because she wanted peace.

She wanted partnership.

She wanted love.

Her silence cost her years of income, assets, and emotional security.

Simple Truth:

Boundaries protect you better than blind trust ever will.

The Story of Amber and Timothy

A Different Pain, the Same Lesson

Amber and Timothy had never lived a flashy life, but they lived a full one. Four kids, a steady home, bills paid on time, and the kind of love that made the hard days easier. Amber worked from home as a customer service agent, juggling calls between loads of laundry. Timothy worked long, grueling days in construction, sunup to sundown, hands rough, shoulders tired, but always thinking about tomorrow.

He worried constantly about their future.

Not the near future, the far future.

Retirement. Security. Stability for their children.

He didn't want to work on construction sites forever. He dreamed of building something that outlasted him.

One afternoon at work, while wiping sweat from his forehead, Timothy opened up to a coworker he trusted.

"Man, I need to build something. We're doing okay, but okay won't cut it when I'm too old to lift these tools."

His coworker nodded slowly.

"Come with me this weekend. There's a seminar you need to see."

The Seminar That Sold the Dream

Timothy walked into the hotel conference room and felt instantly hopeful. Music playing. Smiling presenters. Big screens with photos of beautiful short-term rentals earning thousands a month.

The pitch was polished:

- "Guaranteed passive income."
- "Hands-off ownership."
- "Properties already purchased and rented."
- "Earn $2,000 to $7,000 a month depending on your investment level."
- The idea seemed simple:
- You invest. They manage.
- You collect checks.
- He came home energized, eyes bright, heart racing.
- "Amber," he said, "this is it. This is how we build real wealth."
- And she believed in him. She always had.

So when he withdrew $75,000 from his 401(k) and handed it to the company, she didn't argue. She trusted he was leading them toward a better future.

The Investment That Looked Real, Until It Didn't

A home was purchased shortly after. Timothy's name appeared on a few internal documents, but when he asked about the mortgage or official ownership paperwork, the partner brushed it off.

"Everything is under the corporate umbrella," he said.

"We do it this way for efficiency."

Monthly summaries came in, showing small profits.

$500 one month. $1,000 another.

Then two months with nothing.

The reports never matched what they were promised. Line items for:

- "Cleaning fees"
- "Maintenance charges"
- "Administrative expenses" began to feel excessive.

Amber's gut twisted every time she read them.

"This doesn't look right, Tim."

But Timothy wanted to believe. He wanted to trust that he hadn't made a mistake with their entire retirement fund.

The Moment Everything Became Clear

Tax season arrived, and Timothy took the paperwork to a tax professional, hoping for clarity.

But clarity didn't come.

The accountant flipped through the papers and frowned.

"Where's your partnership agreement?"

"Where are your income statements?"

"Where's proof you own the property?"

"Where's the K-1?"

Timothy had none of it.

His heart dropped.

That night, he confronted the investment partner, demanding answers.

The partner smiled like everything was fine.

"It's all part of the structure," he said.

"You don't need individual documents. The company holds the assets. We minimize taxes with depreciation strategies. Trust me, it's working."

Timothy wanted to believe him.

Amber didn't.

She pressed harder. Called. Emailed. Requested paperwork. Demanded transparency.

Her persistence forced the partner to finally act:

- He created an LLC
- Added them as 50/50 partners
- Opened a joint account for rental deposits and expenses
- Sent a Schedule K-1 at year-end

But still, no closing documents.

Amber wanted to know exactly where their $75,000 went.

Did it buy the property? Or did it simply disappear?

No explanation ever came. Not a single receipt. Not a single closing statement. Finally, the truth was unavoidable.

They needed a lawyer.

And just like that, they were paying even more money, this time for legal help to chase an investment that may have never existed the way it was sold to them.

The wealth-building dream transformed into a financial nightmare.

Business Lessons Told Through Their Story

Simple. Human. Real.

These lessons aren't bullet points.

They are moments in Amber and Timothy's life that every entrepreneur should learn from.

Lesson 1: The Presentation Is the Performance, The Paperwork Is the Truth

When Timothy walked into that seminar, everything looked polished and convincing.

The room felt successful.

The speakers sounded trustworthy.

But contracts, not charisma, protect your money.

If there's no partnership agreement, no written terms, no property documents, you're not investing.

You're gambling.

Lesson 2: Access Is Ownership, If You Can't See It, You Don't Own It

For a whole year, Timothy didn't have:

- Access to bank accounts
- Access to the mortgage
- Access to real financial details
- Access to ownership records

Anything you invest in should give you real visibility.

No access equals no ownership.

Lesson 3: If the Numbers Don't Make Sense, They Aren't Right

Real estate should bring steady returns.

Consistency. Predictability.

But their "profits" bounced around with no logic.

Fees popped up out of nowhere.

Income disappeared and reappeared without explanation.

When the math doesn't match the marketing, a problem is hiding behind the curtain.

Lesson 4: Retirement Is Not a Risk Fund

Withdrawing from a 401(k) comes with:

- Taxes
- Penalties
- Irreversible losses
- Timothy didn't just invest money.

He invested his future.

Never risk retirement funds on promises, only proof.

Lesson 5: The Partner Who Avoids Your Questions Is Answering Them

Every time Amber pushed, the partner dodged. Every time she asked for documents, he gave excuses.

Every time they confronted him, he smoothed it over with charm. A real partner answers questions directly.

A scammer answers with distractions.

Lesson 6: When Something Doesn't Feel Right, Pause, Then Verify

Amber's instincts were strong from the beginning.

But trust made them hesitate. Your gut is a business tool.

Use it. Protect it. Listen to it.

When something feels off, it is.

Final Thought

Hope Is Not a Business Plan

Amber and Timothy didn't fail because they were careless.

They failed because they trusted hope more than documentation.

They believed in the dream, not the details. They followed the promise, not the proof.

And that's the mistake business owners make every day.

The dream is beautiful. The paperwork is essential.

Before investing, partnering, or signing:

- Slow down
- Verify everything
- Demand paperwork
- Ask the uncomfortable questions
- Protect the money you worked for

Because the cost of not knowing is always higher than the cost of finding out.

Chapter Four
Betrayed by Blood

A Story told by local news of Trust, Family, and an Unthinkable Loss

After a lifetime of sacrifice, an elderly couple in their seventies finally reached a season of rest. Their days were simple, morning coffee on the porch, afternoon walks through the neighborhood, and evenings filled with quiet conversation or old photo albums. They lived in the same modest home they purchased decades earlier. It wasn't fancy, but it was theirs, paid off in full, filled with memories, and carrying every laugh, argument, holiday, and milestone of their marriage.

The home was aging, though. The roof leaked during storms.

The kitchen cabinets were splintering.

The bathrooms, once bright, were now stained and outdated.

Wanting to make the repairs but not take on overwhelming debt, the husband decided to pull a small amount of equity from the home, just enough to fix things and enjoy their retirement comfortably.

And he turned to the one person he trusted almost as much as his wife, his grandson.

A young man he helped raise.

A young man he adored.

A young man, he believed, would never hurt him.

The grandson agreed without hesitation.

"Grandpa, don't worry," he said confidently. "Let me handle everything."

The Illusion of Help

A couple of weeks later, the grandson returned with paperwork in hand.

"Just sign these," he said. "It's all for the home equity loan."

The elderly couple signed without reading. They didn't think they needed to.

This was their grandson, blood of their blood.

Not long after, he handed them a check for $20,000 and said everything was approved. They were relieved, grateful, and excited. For the first time in years, they felt like their home could be restored to the warm haven it once was.

Their grandson kept showing up, bringing food, taking them to dinner, smiling, laughing, building what felt like an even stronger bond.

It felt like love. It felt like loyalty. It felt like family.

The Warning No One Wants to Hear

One warm afternoon, while the husband was tending the garden, a neighbor walked over, worry written across her face.

"I've seen a lot of unfamiliar people going in and out of your house," she whispered. "I think someone is showing it to buyers."

The husband froze.

Buyers? Showing the house?

He told his wife. She frowned, confused, but both brushed it off. Maybe the grandson had friends visiting. Maybe they misunderstood. And even if something was going on, this was family.

Family doesn't do that. Right?

The Unthinkable Truth

Months later, an envelope arrived, thick, sealed, and official.

A notice of sale. Not a notice of a loan.

A notice that the home, their fully paid-off home, had been sold.

They had unknowingly signed documents transferring ownership to their grandson.

He had then:

- used the house as collateral
- taken a large loan
- sold the property
- and disappeared

He left the country without a word.

The house where they raised their children.

The home they worked their entire lives to pay off.

The property they trusted their grandson to protect.

Was gone. And so was he.

The couple was left with nothing but heartbreak, a stack of legal notices, and the crushing reality that the person they trusted most had betrayed them completely.

Lessons Hidden in Their Pain

Their story isn't just about a home. It's about decisions, trust, and protection. Every business owner needs to understand these lessons, because betrayal doesn't always come from strangers.

Sometimes it comes from people you love.

Lesson 1: When You Sign Blindly, You Give Away Power

The couple signed papers they didn't read because trust replaced caution.

But signatures are binding, even when the intention isn't.

Story Reminder:

If someone hands you documents and says, "Just sign," stop.

Love doesn't make paperwork safer.

Understanding makes it safer.

Lesson 2: Titles Tell the Truth, Look Before You Lose

They believed they were applying for a loan.

Instead, they signed paperwork transferring ownership.

Had they checked the title or asked to see the deed, the truth would have been clear.

Story Reminder:

Whether it's a home, a business, or a partnership,

ownership is proven on paper, not through relationships.

Lesson 3: Trust Is Beautiful, but Verification Is Protection

They trusted their grandson because of history, not because of paperwork.

But business, big or small, requires proof.

Story Reminder:

You don't verify because you expect betrayal.

You verify so you can prevent it.

Lesson 4: Help Without Boundaries Can Become Harm

The couple asked for help, but without setting limits:

- No oversight
- No attorney
- No review

• No second opinion

That freedom gave their grandson the power to take everything.

Story Reminder:

Whether hiring a bookkeeper, signing with a partner, or seeking financial help, support should come with boundaries and supervision.

Lesson 5: The Most Dangerous Fraud Is the One You Never Expect

We expect deception from strangers.

But fraud from family? That cuts deeper.

And it happens more often than people think.

Story Reminder:

Never assume someone wouldn't do something harmful just because they share your bloodline.

Emotions don't override the need for legal protection.

Lesson 6: Always Have a Legal Ally, Especially in Your Later Years

An attorney reviewing their documents would have taken minutes.

That simple step would have saved their home.

Story Reminder:

For big decisions, real estate, investments, and loans, a legal review is not optional.

It's essential.

Final Thought

Love Should Never Replace Legal Protection

This couple's story is heartbreaking, but it teaches a powerful truth:

Trust is emotional. Protection is practical.

Whether you're elderly, a new entrepreneur, or a seasoned business owner:

- Ask questions
- Read everything
- Get documents reviewed
- Understand ownership
- Set boundaries, even with family
- Protect your legacy

Because betrayal doesn't just cost money.

It can cost your peace, your security, and everything you spent a lifetime building.

And as harsh as it sounds:

Trust is earned.

But verification is how you keep what you earned.

When Loyalty Costs More Than Labor

The Story

José came to the United States at a young age, full of hope and determination. He first landed in sunny California, where opportunity felt endless for someone willing to work. With no formal education and very little capital, José did what many immigrants do—he hustled.

Every day, José collected discarded pallets, repaired them, and resold them to local companies. The work was exhausting and time-consuming, but he saw what others didn't: demand. He dreamed of one day owning a full pallet yard where businesses would come directly to him for service. José saved every dollar he earned. Slowly, what started as survival became profitable.

Life was good. José met the woman he believed was the love of his life. They married, started a family, and built a modest but stable life. With his wife's encouragement and support, José decided to take the next big step—opening his own pallet yard.

To make it happen, he relocated to Arizona, where land was cheaper and expansion was possible. His wife, however, did not want to leave California. Believing he could manage both responsibilities, José moved alone and began building the business from the ground up.

He worked tirelessly—handling production in the yard while hiring an office manager to oversee administrative work and cash collections. As the business grew, José made a personal mistake that would change everything. He became involved with the office manager, who later became pregnant. José was still married, and worse, he soon discovered the woman struggled with drug addiction—something he had not known.

Despite the chaos, José continued to provide for his wife and children back in California while growing the business in Arizona. But behind the scenes, the office manager was stealing cash from the business to fund her addiction. When it became clear she was unfit to care for the child, José terminated her employment and forced her to leave the business. She walked away—but left the child behind.

José raised the little girl as his own.

He brought her to work every day. She grew up in the pallet yard, learning the business by watching him. José poured love into her and into the company. Together, they grew the operation. The business thrived.

But time passed.

The little girl became a teenager, and at 19, she became pregnant. Wanting to protect her and give her stability, José placed her in an apartment and continued supporting her financially. Around the same time, the office manager José had hired to replace the previous one began clashing with his daughter. One day, she quit without notice.

Suddenly, José was without financial oversight.

Needing someone he trusted, José placed his daughter in charge of the office and daily money handling. That decision proved costly. Over time, she began using the business account like a personal checking account—paying bills, covering expenses, and withdrawing cash without accountability.

This time, José took action.

He hired an accountant who didn't just clean up the books—she transformed the business. She became his CFO. She implemented structure, monitored every transaction, and created systems for accountability. Payroll was established. Employees were converted properly and given benefits. The company introduced 401(k) plans and medical insurance. Profits soared.

The business became so stable that CFO visits were reduced to once a month.

Then the numbers started to change.

Profits declined. Clients quietly left. Cash flow tightened. The CFO returned full-time to investigate and uncovered the issue: José's son had joined the business and begun making operational decisions without structure or oversight. At the same time, extended family members were regularly requesting financial help—rent, debts, legal trouble. José paid for it all, pulling money directly from the business.

The CFO warned him clearly:

This is destroying your cash flow.

José listened—for a while. The business stabilized again.

But old habits returned. Family influence crept back in. Decisions were made emotionally instead of strategically. Control slipped away. What was once a company generating $200,000–$300,000 per month dropped to $90,000 per month.

José didn't lose everything—but he lost momentum, stability, and control.

And today, he is still rebuilding—learning the painful cost of allowing family to control the destiny of a business he worked his entire life to build.

The Business Lessons

José's story is not about lack of effort—it's about lack of boundaries.

1. Trust Without Oversight Is a Liability

Whether it's a spouse, child, or employee, no one should handle cash or financial decisions without checks and controls.

2. Family and Business Must Have Clear Lines

Good intentions do not replace structure. Family members must earn roles, follow rules, and be held accountable like anyone else.

3. Emotional Decisions Drain Profitable Businesses

Helping family is admirable—but doing it through the business destroys cash flow and sustainability.

4. One Strong CFO Can Change Everything

Structure, payroll, benefits, and monitoring saved José's business—proof that professional oversight matters.

5. Revenue Does Not Equal Stability

High monthly income means nothing if profits are leaking through poor controls and unchecked access.

6. Leadership Requires Saying No

Protecting the business sometimes means disappointing the people you love.

Conclusion

José's life is a testament to hard work, resilience, and vision—but also a warning.

He built something powerful from nothing. But by allowing personal relationships to override structure, he handed control of his destiny to others. Success didn't disappear overnight—it eroded slowly, decision by decision.

José is still standing. Still working. Still rebuilding.

But his greatest lesson is clear:

You cannot save everyone and still save your business.

Structure is not selfish. Boundaries are not betrayal. And protecting your business is the only way to protect your future.

Because when you allow others to control your business, you allow them to control your success.

Final Conclusion: When Love Replaces Structure

Chapter Four reveals a truth many people don't want to confront: **the deepest betrayals often come from the closest relationships**.

The elderly couple lost their home not because they were careless, but because they believed blood guaranteed protection. José nearly lost everything he built because loyalty to family outweighed discipline and boundaries. In both stories, the common thread is painfully clear—**trust was given freely, but structure was missing**.

Neither story began with bad intentions.
Both began with love, sacrifice, and good faith.

But love does not review documents.
Loyalty does not manage cash flow.
And family ties do not replace legal authority or financial controls.

The couple believed their grandson would protect their legacy. Instead, they unknowingly signed it away. José believed caring for family through his business would keep everyone safe. Instead, it slowly drained the very foundation meant to support them all.

What these stories teach is not to distrust family—but to **stop confusing love with protection**.

Protection looks like:

- Reading every document
- Verifying ownership
- Separating personal needs from business funds
- Assigning roles based on qualifications, not relationships
- Enforcing boundaries even when it's uncomfortable

Legacy is not preserved through emotion—it is preserved through structure.

Both the couple and José worked their entire lives to build something meaningful. And both learned, at a high cost, that **what you build can be taken from you when you hand control to the wrong hands—intentionally or not**.

The lesson of this chapter is simple, but heavy:

You can love deeply and still protect yourself.
You can help family without sacrificing your future.
And you can honor relationships without surrendering control.

Because in business—and in life—
trust without verification is not kindness.
It is risk.

And risk, when unmanaged, can cost you everything you spent a lifetime building.

Chapter 5
When Loyalty Blinds Judgment

Linda had always been a bright light in the corporate world. She was the kind of leader who lifted people up instead of tearing them down. As a controller at a large company, she managed millions with ease, but handled people with even greater care.

Her famous saying echoed through every department:

"If my staff made a mistake, that means I didn't train them properly."

She meant it. She lived it.

And because of it, she became the kind of leader people would follow anywhere.

Her loyalty earned her trust.

Her compassion earned her influence. Her work ethic earned her promotions.

But the same loyalty that made her remarkable soon made her vulnerable.

The Friend She Tried to Save

One afternoon, Linda met an old friend for lunch. The woman looked nothing like the confident person she once knew. Her eyes were tired, her voice shaky as she shared her struggles.

Her marriage was collapsing. Her finances were in ruins.

She needed a job, not just for income, but for survival.

Moved by her friend's pain, Linda pleaded with the company owners:

"Give her a chance. I'll take responsibility."

Despite hesitation, they agreed.

The friend was hired as Accounting Manager, earning $50,000 a year. This was more than the owners wanted to offer, but they trusted Linda's judgment.

The friend took Linda's former seat.

Linda was moved into an isolated management office away from the staff she adored.

At first, everything seemed fine.

Then four months passed. And everything changed.

The Shift That No One Expected

The friend Linda fought so hard to protect started acting like someone else entirely.

She dressed inappropriately. She disrespected the staff.

She created tension everywhere she went.

One accounts payable clerk even quit because of her, returning only when Linda personally intervened.

Then life hit hard.

Linda's sister became ill, and Linda left town for two weeks to care for her.

When she returned, the atmosphere at work felt different.

Cold. Distant. Suspicious.

She noticed whispers. Side glances.

A strange shift in leadership's tone.

But the worst blow came quietly.

Linda discovered her job had been posted online.

Her heart dropped. Her stomach knotted.

The betrayal was quiet, but sharp.

Still, she pushed through, kept working, and began looking for other opportunities privately.

The Betrayal Behind the Smile

When Linda finally got a promising interview out of state, she confided in the one person she believed she could trust, her friend.

"Please don't say anything," she whispered.

Her friend nodded, claiming loyalty.

Days later, one of the owners confronted Linda:

"So, what's this day off you need for an 'appointment'?"

Linda froze. Only one person knew.

Her friend. The betrayal was undeniable.

And things spiraled from there. Meetings became uncomfortable.

Leadership seemed agitated.

The work environment grew hostile.

Linda quietly packed her things.

But before she could leave, the owner stopped her.

"Don't make any decisions today," he said.

"Let me handle this."

The Day Everything Came to Light

At the next team lunch, the owner made a major announcement.

A company restructuring. Linda was reinstated.

Her former responsibilities were restored.

Control returned to her hands.

Her friend, however, was demoted to Accounts Receivable Manager.

The shock on her face said everything. Betrayal has a way of circling back home.

A month later, the friend quit, with no notice and no goodbye.

But the damage wasn't over.

The Hidden Sabotage

Even after leaving, the friend kept calling Linda, asking:

"Where are you interviewing?"

"What's next for you?"

Linda, being naturally open and trusting, answered.

But soon she noticed odd things happening at interviews.

Questions about her old company. Unusual hesitations.

Strange comments that didn't align with her resume.

It didn't take long to realize her former friend was calling around, undermining her, poisoning her reputation, and making her road harder on purpose.

That was the final straw.

Linda stopped sharing everything.

She detached emotionally. She closed the door and locked it.

Months later, they ran into each other at a birthday party. Linda calmly told her truth, softly, firmly, and without anger.

"I forgive you.

But we can't be friends anymore."

It was closure. Not reconciliation.

When Entrepreneurship Reveals Another Betrayal

Life eventually guided Linda into new leadership roles and, finally, into entrepreneurship. She opened her own firm, a place built on trust, integrity, and fairness. She hired people she believed in and gave them freedom and flexibility.

One day, she traveled to volunteer, leaving a trusted employee in charge.

When she returned, her phone was full of client cancellations.

Something felt off.

She contacted one client, who explained that another firm was offering them a better deal. But something didn't sit right about that firm. Their credentials were unclear. Their promises felt suspicious.

The truth finally surfaced. The employee she trusted was behind it all.

Recruiting her clients. Undercutting her.

Trying to steal her business while she was away.

Linda confronted the situation with strength and grace.

She reached out, reclaimed many of her clients, but told them:

"If you were willing to leave based on unethical outreach, I can't continue working with you."

She returned their records and let them go, choosing integrity over income.

Once again, trust cost her something. But she rebuilt. She healed.

And she succeeded anyway.

Lessons Wrapped in the Story

Simple, Human, and Easy for Any Business Owner to Apply

These lessons aren't abstract bullet points. They're lived moments from Linda's journey, told in ways every entrepreneur can understand.

Lesson 1: Compassion Is Beautiful, but It Can Blind You

Linda hired her friend from a place of love.

But business requires evaluation, not emotion.

Story Reminder:

Helping someone is kind.

Hiring someone is a business decision.

Never mix the two without clarity.

Lesson 2: Loyalty Without Boundaries Becomes a Liability

Linda trusted too easily.

Shared too openly.

Believed too deeply.

And that loyalty gave others power to hurt her.

Story Reminder:

Protect your heart, but guard your business.

Lesson 3: Silence Isn't Privacy, It's Protection

When Linda shared her interview plans, it cost her opportunities.

Not everyone who listens supports you.

Story Reminder:

Your next move is safest when it's quiet.

Lesson 4: Time Away Reveals the Truth

When Linda left to care for her sister, her absence created space for betrayal to take root.

When she later left town for volunteer work, an employee attempted to take her clients.

Story Reminder:

Leadership requires systems, not just trust.

Your business should run ethically, even when you aren't looking.

Lesson 5: A Friend at Work Is Still an Employee in the Business

Lines blurred.

Roles blurred.

Expectations blurred.

And accountability became impossible.

Story Reminder:

Hire friends only if you can also fire them.

If you can't, don't hire them.

Lesson 6: When Someone Shows You Who They Are, Believe It

Betrayal came twice.

Different people.

Different situations.

Same pattern.

Story Reminder:

A broken pattern is a conscious choice.

A repeated one is a warning.

Lesson 7: Reputation Is Fragile, Protect It Fiercely

Linda discovered people were questioning her credibility because of rumors.

Instead of hiding, she confronted it with clarity and professionalism.

Story Reminder:

Your reputation is your business currency.

Guard it the way you guard your bank account.

Lesson 8: Forgiveness Is Peace, but Reconnection Is Optional

Linda forgave, but she did not go back.

Forgiveness healed her heart, not her boundaries.

Story Reminder:

Forgive people and free yourself, but you never have to reopen access to your life.

Closing Thought

Not Everyone You Save Will Protect You

Linda's story is a reminder that loyalty, while admirable, must be paired with wisdom.

Some people enter your life as lessons.

Some enter as blessings.

Some enter as warnings you must learn to recognize.

But in business and in life, your peace, your reputation, and your future deserve more protection than your emotions.

Move wisely. Lead cautiously.

And always remember:

Loyalty is earned.

Trust is verified.

And rebuilding is always possible, no matter who tried to break you.

When Passion Meets Poor Partnerships

Cynthia's Story

Cynthia had always loved the kitchen. Long before she dreamed of owning a restaurant, she was that friend who showed up at every event with a dish people begged her to make again. She cooked with feeling. With memory. With heart.

Her neighbors knew it. Her coworkers knew it.

Her family definitely knew it.

As her food grew more popular, her confidence grew too. What started as small weekend orders soon became a steady stream of customers knocking on her door, asking:

"Are you cooking this week?"

And like most dreamers, Cynthia started imagining more.

A menu of her own. A restaurant with her name on it.

A place where her passion could live and breathe.

But dreams don't build themselves.

And dreams built with the wrong people can cost everything.

The Partnership That Looked Promising

With demand rising, Cynthia partnered with three individuals who claimed to share her excitement. They talked big. They shared ideas. They promised teamwork.

And Cynthia believed them.

Together, they opened a small restaurant with a focused, curated menu. The place was clean and trendy with that "hidden gem" feel customers loved. They were listed on delivery apps. Reviews rolled in. People talked about the food. And from the outside, it looked like a success story in the making.

But Cynthia lived a double life. A full-time job during the day. A restaurant owner at night.

She worked late evenings, helped with prep, built the brand, created recipes, and poured every extra dollar into the business. Meanwhile, her partners claimed they were handling daily operations.

At least, that's what they said they were doing.

The First Red Flags

Even with customers coming in and payments flowing through the POS system, the business was always short on cash.

Always. Payroll came up short.

Vendors needed payments.

Unexpected "emergencies" happened weekly.

More than once, Cynthia reached into her own pocket, pulling out thousands of dollars at a time to keep the doors open.

Concerned but still believing in the dream, she obtained a line of credit from the bank.

But something didn't sit right. Each week, she checked the balance.

Each week, the line of credit was drained again.

"What happened to all the sales?"

"Why are we always broke?"

"Where is the money going?"

Her partners never gave real answers. Only promises to "get things under control."

But nothing changed.

The Truth Hiding in the Books

Finally, out of frustration and fear, Cynthia hired a CPA to produce the financial reports the bank needed for a loan.

That was when everything began to unravel.

The CPA compared the POS reports to the bank deposits and frowned.

"Cynthia, these numbers don't match at all."

In one month, the POS showed $40,000 in sales.

But only $15,000 was deposited into the bank.

The rest was:

Gone. Missing. Unaccounted for.

When she confronted her partners, they brushed it off.

"Oh, we used the cash to buy inventory."

"We needed supplies."

"It's normal."

But the CPA didn't buy it.

He pointed to duplicated transactions.

Strange reversals. Inconsistent food costs.

Numbers that simply didn't add up.

His final words hit Cynthia like a punch:

"Someone is mismanaging or misusing your money.

Deeply."

Love, Loyalty, and a Costly Blind Spot

Cynthia was devastated, not just by the numbers, but by what she finally had to admit.

She had been emotionally involved with one of her partners.

And because of that relationship, she ignored the warning signs.

Ignored her instincts.

Ignored her growing discomfort.

Love blurred her judgment. Loyalty silenced her questions.

And her silence cost her control.

Trying to Rebuild, Only to Be Hit Again

Cynthia ended the relationship.

Ended the business partnership.

With the CPA's help, she secured a bank loan to save the restaurant and start fresh.

But before she could stabilize the business, another betrayal surfaced.

One former partner took:

- her recipes
- her menu design
- her business concept
- an almost identical name to hers

He opened a competing restaurant less than twenty minutes away.

Customers began drifting toward the copycat business.

Her dream, once vibrant and exciting, was slowly being stripped away.

Cynthia is still rebuilding. Still recovering. Still trying to heal from the financial and emotional wreckage left behind.

She still loves food. She still has the gift.

But trust is now something she guards fiercely.

Lessons from Cynthia's Journey

Simple, Human, and Told Through the Story Itself

Lesson 1: Passion Needs Protection, Not Just Partners

Cynthia believed enthusiasm was enough to build a strong team.

But passion doesn't prove integrity.

Excitement doesn't prove ethics.

Story Reminder:

Before you build with someone, research them.

Verify them.

Understand their track record.

Partnerships should be earned, never assumed.

Lesson 2: Never Mix Business With Romance Without Safeguards

Her emotional involvement clouded her ability to question the numbers.

Story Reminder:

Business needs clear eyes, not blurred lines.

Love is emotional.

Contracts are protection.

Always keep the two separate.

Lesson 3: Monitor the Money as If Your Business Depends on It, Because It Does

Cynthia's biggest blind spot was letting others manage the daily finances.

By the time she checked, the damage was deep.

Story Reminder:

Even if you're busy, you must implement:

- weekly financial reviews
- bank reconciliation oversight
- transparent reporting systems
- third-party audits

Your eyes should always be on the cash.

Lesson 4: POS Numbers Mean Nothing Without Bank Reconciliation

The business looked busy.

Orders were flowing.

Reviews were great.

But the bank account told the truth.

Story Reminder:

Compare sales to deposits every month.

If the numbers don't match, someone is lying.

Lesson 5: Protect Your Recipes, Brand, and Ideas Early

Cynthia trusted her partners with her intellectual property.

They stole it.

Story Reminder:

Your creativity is your currency.

Guard it with:

- trademarks
- copyrights
- NDAs
- recipe protection agreements
- Protect it before you share it.

Lesson 6: X's and O's Don't Equal Ownership

Cynthia invested without maintaining control over:

- the bank accounts
- cash handling
- purchasing authority
- operations

And her partners took advantage of it.

Story Reminder:

If you fund the dream, you must control the money.

Lesson 7: Your Gut Speaks Before Numbers Do, Listen Early

Cynthia felt uneasy long before the CPA confirmed it.

But she waited.

Story Reminder:

Instinct is data.

Don't ignore it.

Final Thought

Passion Builds the Dream, but Protection Keeps It Alive

Cynthia's story is painful, but powerful.

She cooked with love. Created with talent. Built with vision.

But she trusted without verifying. Partnered without protecting.

And allowed passion to overshadow strategy. For every business owner, her story is a reminder:

Your dream deserves more than excitement. It deserves structure, control, and protection.

Because passion may start the business, but wisdom is what keeps it alive.

When Brotherhood Turns into Business Betrayal

Jim & David's Story

Jim and David weren't just friends. They were family in everything but blood. They met in high school, bonded on the basketball court, spent summers together, survived breakups together, celebrated wins together, and built a brotherhood people envied. They were side by side through life's biggest moments, so when adulthood arrived, going into business together felt natural.

Jim came from a financially stable home. His parents were well off, supportive, and able to help him get started in life. David didn't have the same financial advantage, but what he lacked in resources, he made up for with grit, heart, and an unstoppable work ethic.

Together, they created their first venture: a youth sports training program.

It wasn't a gold mine, but it had a purpose. They trained young athletes, helped them develop discipline, and built a safe space for kids who needed direction. It gave them joy. It gave them meaning. And it deepened their bond.

Then one day, David came to Jim with not one, but two big ideas.

The Ideas That Sparked Everything

David had been thinking. He knew they had something special, and he saw ways to take their business to the next level.

Idea One:

A new piece of training equipment he designed, something unique, something effective, something that could change the way young athletes trained.

Idea Two:

A mobile app that allowed athletes to track their skills, monitor their progress, and stay engaged long after they left the facility.

He pitched both ideas to Jim with excitement, passion, and hope.

Jim agreed. The ideas were brilliant.

“We’ll work on it together,” he promised.

But weeks passed. Then months passed. And nothing happened.

Whenever David brought up the ideas, Jim brushed him off:

“I’ve been busy.”

“We’ll get to it soon.”

“Let’s meet next week.”

Next week never came.

The Beginning of the Shift

Eventually, David insisted they sit down to talk seriously. They met at a restaurant, and Jim delivered the news:

“I’m going in a different direction. I met someone, and I’m focused on building a future with her.”

David was hurt, but he tried to be supportive. He understood that love changes priorities.

He even asked to meet Jim's new partner, and Jim invited him to a party he was hosting.

At the party, David mingled with old friends and new acquaintances. He noticed Jim was distracted, present physically but not emotionally. Their paths were clearly diverging, but David still hoped they would find a way to work together again.

When it became clear Jim was pulling away, David stayed committed to their youth training program and eventually brought on a new partner to help continue the mission.

Life moved on. Or so David thought.

The News That Stopped Him Cold

A few months later, mutual friends reached out with surprising news:

"Jim opened a new business. It's doing really well."

David was confused.

Why hadn't Jim told him? Why was Jim avoiding his calls? What direction had he taken?

With no answers from Jim, David visited Jim's parents to ask where the new facility was located.

What he walked into nearly knocked the breath out of him.

The Ultimate Betrayal

The moment David stepped through the doors of Jim's new business, his heart dropped.

Everything he saw belonged to him.

Not legally, but morally.

Creatively. Conceptually. The equipment. The layouts. The technology. The app features.

Everything David had shared, every idea and every dream, had been brought to life.

Just without him.

As he walked across the training floor in disbelief, Jim approached him casually, as if nothing was wrong.

"Hey man," Jim said. "Didn't expect to see you."

David's voice trembled.

"How could you take my ideas and open this place without me?"

Jim didn't flinch.

"You didn't have the resources," he said.

"Neither did I. So I found investors. They would only work with me, not us. I had to make a decision based on my future."

It was cold. Calculated. Cruel.

David realized in that moment that his best friend had never been building a business with him.

Jim had been studying him. Using him. Extracting value.

Then, moving on to the moment something better came along.

That day, their decades-long brotherhood ended.

They never spoke again.

David walked away with anger, heartbreak, and a sense of loss deeper than any business failure. He didn't just lose a business idea.

He lost family.

Lessons Written in the Story

Simple. Human. And Easy for Business Owners to Learn From

Lesson 1: Great Ideas Need More Than Excitement, They Need Protection

David shared his ideas freely, trusting their history.

But creativity without documentation is vulnerable.

Ideas without agreements are unprotected.

Verbal promises don't hold up in business.

Story Reminder:

Passion is powerful.

Documentation is protection.

Lesson 2: Friendship Does Not Automatically Make Someone a Business Partner

David assumed brotherhood equaled loyalty.

Jim assumed opportunity equaled ownership.

Friendship is emotional.

Business is strategic.

Without structure, even the strongest bonds can break.

Story Reminder:

Friends can be part of your support system,

but business requires contracts, clarity, and boundaries.

Lesson 3: Expectations Not Communicated Become Expectations Not Met

David thought they were building together.

Jim had already moved on.

Assumptions are dangerous in business,

especially when money, ownership, and ideas are involved.

Story Reminder:

Speak it. Write it. Clarify it.

Don't guess where someone stands.

Lesson 4: Power Shifts When One Person Controls the Money

Jim funded their first project.

That dynamic gave him leverage.

Leverage eventually became betrayal.

Balanced resources create balanced partnerships.

Story Reminder:

Never build a dream where you have no financial or strategic control.

Lesson 5: When Ideas Matter, Track Where They Come From

David never documented the development of the equipment or app.

No notes. No drafts. No email trails.

Jim took advantage.

Story Reminder:

Put your ideas in writing.

Protect your design process.

Own your innovation.

Lesson 6: Betrayal Is Often a Beginning, Not the End

David lost a friendship and a business vision.

But he walked away with something Jim didn't have:

Integrity, clarity, and the strength to rebuild the right way.

Painful endings often make room for better beginnings.

Story Reminder:

Sometimes the door that closes is protecting you from a future you were never meant to share.

Final Thought

The Cost of Unprotected Trust

Jim and David's story carries the same message as Linda's, Cynthia's, and others:

Betrayal doesn't always come from outside your circle.

Sometimes it comes from the people you trust most.

Their stories share the same pattern:

- loyalty given too freely
- boundaries left unspoken
- ideas shared without protection
- partnerships formed without clarity
- These aren't just business fumbles.
- They are emotional wounds that derail dreams.
- But they also prove something powerful:
- People may fail you.

- But resilience never will.
- So guard your ideas.
- Protect your partnerships.
- Honor your vision.
- And never let loyalty blind your business judgment.
- Because your dream deserves more than trust.
- It deserves strategy, protection, and wisdom.

The Cost of Trust Without Structure

The Story

Stacy was born curious, confident, and adored. Raised in a small family with just one brother, she was the only girl—and she was treated like royalty. Her parents and uncles surrounded her with affection, protection, and praise. From an early age, Stacy learned she was special, and she carried that belief with her into adulthood.

She was strong-willed and independent, often resisting guidance from her mother because she preferred learning life on her own terms. As she grew older, her beauty and confidence attracted attention effortlessly. Men admired her, spoiled her, and reinforced the narrative she had always known—she was meant to be cherished, protected, and provided for.

In high school, Stacy fell in with the wrong crowd—people who understood how charm and influence could be exchanged for money, gifts, and opportunity. Attention came easily. Money followed just as quickly. Eventually, Stacy entered the club scene as a dancer, where she earned significant income by mastering one powerful truth: she knew how to make people feel wanted—and people paid generously for that feeling.

Years later, Stacy met a man she believed was her knight in shining armor. Ignoring countless red flags, she married him. Wanting to prove her loyalty and commitment, she paid for the wedding, supported their lifestyle, bought herself a car—and bought him a Corvette. He wore success but never earned it. When Stacy became pregnant and could no longer work, reality hit hard. There was no backup plan. No savings. No partner stepping up.

The marriage ended quickly—and painfully—but it became her first real wake-up call.

Stacy returned to the lifestyle she knew, doing what she had always done to survive and provide. Over time, she realized she possessed something more enduring than beauty—she had vision. She could see opportunity where others couldn't and turn ideas into reality.

Eventually, Stacy met another man—one she believed truly saw her value. He was a personal trainer: disciplined, ambitious, and focused on health. She felt they were aligned in mindset and goals. When she shared her vision of starting a healthy food and meal prep business, he loved the idea. To Stacy, this wasn't just a business—it was a shared future. They married, relocated to a new state, and committed to building their empire together.

Because she wanted the marriage to work, Stacy believed a formal contract wasn't necessary. In her mind, paperwork created division. She didn't want "his business" and "her business"—she wanted *their* business. She trusted that love, marriage, and shared purpose were enough. She believed that building together meant trusting completely.

Stacy poured herself into the venture. She created healthy, convenient meals customers loved. She started small, prepping meals for her husband's training clients, then expanded. She developed pricing, perfected recipes, built relationships with schools and organizations, and even helped create an app so customers could order meals for the entire week.

Her days started early in the kitchen and ended late with planning and relationship-building. Orders increased. Revenue flowed. On the surface, Stacy's life finally looked like the dream she had always imagined.

But slowly, things began to change.

Her husband started hiring staff—then managers. He encouraged Stacy to rest more. Then he told her others would handle operations. Piece by piece, she was pushed out of the business she had built. When Stacy questioned him, he accused her of doing nothing, of being a burden.

Confused and alarmed, Stacy hired an accountant to review the finances. The numbers didn't add up. Based on food costs and margins, there should have been far more money in the bank. The accountant explained that revenue appeared to be missing—likely pocketed.

When Stacy confronted her husband, he casually admitted that much of the business income was collected in cash—payments from gym clients, deliveries, and local stores—and never deposited.

Then came the blow that shattered everything.

He told her the business wasn't hers. Her name had been removed from the company and the bank accounts. Staff had been told she no longer worked there. Shortly after, he packed a suitcase, walked out, and ended the marriage.

Stacy was devastated. She was isolated in a state far from family, with children to support and no income. But one thing saved her—relationships. The accountant stood by her. Friends helped her return home. Former clients promised to work with her again once she restarted.

Stacy started over.

A year after she left, the business she built without her collapsed.

The Business Lesson

Stacy's story is not about love gone wrong—it is about **trust without structure**.

Her greatest mistake was not believing in marriage or partnership. Her mistake was believing that commitment alone could replace documentation. She wanted unity, not division. She wanted to build *together*, not prepare for separation. And because of that, she ignored the systems designed to protect her.

Stacy made three critical errors:

1. **She confused contribution with ownership.**
   Vision, labor, and sacrifice do not equal ownership unless they are legally documented.
2. **She trusted love over structure.**
   Marriage does not automatically grant business rights. Love does not override operating agreements, bank access, or legal authority.
3. **She allowed access without accountability.**
   Cash businesses are high-risk environments. Without controls, oversight, and transparency, money disappears—and so does power.

Entrepreneurs must understand this hard truth:
Wanting a relationship to work does not mean you stop protecting yourself.

A strong foundation does not weaken a partnership—it strengthens it. Clear roles, documented ownership, and financial controls do not create distance. They create security.

If your name is not on the entity, the bank account, and the operating agreement, you do not own the business—no matter how hard you worked.

Conclusion

Stacy lost a business—but she gained clarity.

She learned that being loyal does not mean being unprotected. That trust should never come at the cost of structure. And that building an empire together requires more than love—it requires intention, documentation, and financial literacy.

Stacy didn't fail because she trusted.

She failed because she trusted **without boundaries**.

What ultimately saved her was what no one could take away: her experience, her resilience, and her ability to rebuild smarter.

This time, she understood the crown she wore was not symbolic—it was strategic.

And this time, she built it right.

Chapter 6
When Living for the Moment Costs You the Future

Samantha never thought of herself as irresponsible. She simply lived life the way she had always known: make money, pay the bills, then enjoy what was left. She discovered her love for hair early, practicing braids and silk presses on family members until she earned her place in beauty school. By her mid-twenties, she was known around town as the stylist with the magic hands.

Clients followed her from salon to salon until she eventually opened her own shop. It was small but charming, and the steady hum of blow dryers filled her with pride. From the outside, she looked like a woman winning in life. But inside the shop, behind the chair, and especially behind closed doors, there was an entirely different story unfolding.

The Pattern That Cost Her Everything

Samantha had developed a risky routine. She booked clients aggressively during the first ten days of the month. She worked sunrise to sunset, hustling hard until she made just enough to cover rent, utilities, her children's needs, and the basics.

Then she shut it all down.

The rest of the month was reserved for partying with friends, weekend trips, endless drinks, and what she proudly called "living my best life."

Her income wasn't low. She simply refused to build discipline around it. She relied on food stamps to help feed her children and often accepted financial favors from the men she dated. When it came to taxes, she filed returns that showed high expenses and very little income. This resulted in large refunds each year due to child tax credits.

In her mind, she had figured out a system that let her avoid struggle.

But what she actually avoided was responsibility.

She never tracked her earnings, rarely saved, and never planned for anything beyond the next weekend. Her business wasn't failing, but it wasn't growing either. It was stagnant, just like her mindset.

The Night Everything Changed

One evening, during another night out, Samantha was involved in a serious accident. Her injuries were severe enough to keep her hospitalized for more than a month. While she was recovering, her children were shuffled between relatives, and her shop sat dark with a "closed until further notice" sign taped to the door.

By the time she was able to walk again, two months had passed.

Rent was overdue. Clients had moved on. Her reputation had slipped.

When she reopened, Samantha tried to rebuild, but her habits never evolved. She returned to the same cycle, working hard only when bills were due and disappearing the moment she met her minimum. The accident taught her nothing.

Years drifted by, and so did Samantha's opportunities.

A Hard Reality at 45

At age 45, Samantha found herself exhausted, frustrated, and terrified. The beauty industry had changed. Younger stylists were more disciplined, more business-savvy, and social-media smart. Meanwhile, Samantha had:

- No retirement
- No savings
- No assets
- No business systems
- No consistent tax filings
- No financial documentation

Seeking guidance, she met with a financial advisor. He asked for profit-and-loss statements, tax returns, and financial records. Samantha had none. She hired a bookkeeper, who pieced together what little she had.

The truth shocked her.

By reporting low income to get larger tax refunds, she had also:

- Underreported her Social Security earnings
- Eliminated her chances of qualifying for a mortgage
- Destroyed her financial credibility
- Missed out on retirement contributions
- Limited her future earning potential

To catch up, she would need to save aggressively, something she had never done before.

For the first time in her life, she realized she had worked for decades but built nothing.

A Mother's Worst Nightmare

Just as Samantha was starting to take her finances seriously, tragedy struck again. Her twelve-year-old son was killed in an accident.

Her world shattered.

As she sat in the funeral home making arrangements, she faced a reality no parent should ever experience: the cost. Between the casket, burial plot, and service, the expenses were overwhelming.

And she had no insurance. No savings. No burial plan. Nothing to stand on.

A GoFundMe eased some of the burden, but it wasn't enough. Samantha had to take on debt just to lay her child to rest. That moment broke her in ways she never fully recovered from.

A close friend later sat with her and gently said, "You have to prepare. Life doesn't wait for us to get our lives together."

Samantha finally listened. She purchased life insurance.

She adjusted her spending. She started saving.

She began living with intention.

But even with all the changes, she often wondered how different her life would look if she had taken her business and her future seriously from the start.

Lessons for Business Owners

1. Treat Your Passion Like a Real Business

Talent isn't enough. Samantha had skills, but inconsistency and poor discipline sabotaged her success. Entrepreneurship requires daily commitment, structure, and accountability.

2. Balance Enjoyment With Responsibility

There is nothing wrong with enjoying life, but not at the expense of your future. Budgeting, saving, and planning must come before celebrations.

3. Be Honest on Your Taxes

Underreporting income for bigger refunds feels good in the moment, but it destroys your long-term financial foundation. Loans, Social Security, retirement, and credibility all depend on accurate reporting.

4. Prepare for the Unexpected

Accidents, illnesses, and emergencies don't wait until we're ready. Every entrepreneur needs:

- An emergency fund
- Insurance
- A backup plan for their business

5. Protect Your Family With Insurance

Life insurance is not optional. It is an act of love and protection, especially for parents. Don't wait until tragedy forces you to learn this lesson.

6. Seek Professional Help Before It's Too Late

Financial advisors, tax professionals, and business consultants exist to guide you. The earlier you get help, the stronger your foundation becomes.

7. Growth Starts With Accountability

Even after decades of unhealthy habits, Samantha chose to rebuild. Change is always possible, but it requires honesty, discipline, and consistency.

Conclusion

Samantha's journey is a powerful reminder that success isn't measured by how much you make. It is measured by what you build. She spent years chasing moments of fun, only to realize she had sacrificed her peace, her future, and her children's financial security.

For every business owner reading this:

Don't let today's comfort steal tomorrow's stability.

Work with intention, plan ahead, protect your family, and build a future you can stand on proudly.

Living for the moment feels good,

but preparing for the future changes your life.

And your children deserve that version of you.

Part Two

When Beauty Blinds the Budget: Natasha's Story

Natasha had always been "the pretty girl." Even in high school, she stood out with flawless skin, long lashes, perfect brows, and a confidence that made people stop mid-sentence. Compliments weren't rare. They were expected. Everywhere she went, someone was trying to win her attention.

So when her mother talked about college applications and scholarship opportunities, Natasha listened politely. But her heart was already elsewhere. A group of girls she admired worked at a local strip club, showing up with new bags, fresh wigs, and thick stacks of cash. Natasha watched them walk through the mall with a confidence that came from one thing: money. Fast money.

One night, she went with them just to see.

By the end of the week, she had auditioned.

By the end of the month, she was making more money than most people earned in a quarter.

Fast Money, Faster Spending

Natasha was an instant hit. She made thousands in a single night and sometimes walked out with $4,000 to $5,000 after a weekend shift. With that kind of income, she didn't think twice about dropping $800 on a hairstyle or paying $250 every week for nails. Designer bags filled her closet faster than she could keep up with them.

She drove luxury cars.

She lived in luxury apartments.

She dated men who could afford her lifestyle, or at least pretended they could.

To the outside world, Natasha looked like success. But behind the glow of Instagram filters and VIP nights was a young woman with no savings, no plan, and no idea where all her money was going.

Motherhood Doesn't Pause the Bills

By her mid-twenties, Natasha had two children, each with a different father. One was incarcerated. The other was inconsistent. Natasha continued dancing, spending, and moving through life one glamorous night at a time.

But as she crossed into her thirties, something shifted. She wanted stability. She wanted a home for her kids. She wanted to transition from the stage to something more secure, but she didn't know how.

Still, she took the first step. She called a realtor.

A Dream Meets Reality

During the pre-approval process, Natasha proudly told the loan officer she made six figures. She submitted bank statements showing hundreds of thousands in deposits. She expected the lender to be impressed.

Instead, they asked a simple question that stopped her cold:

"What's your long-term plan for income when dancing is no longer an option?"

She didn't have an answer because she had never looked that far ahead.

When the mortgage was denied, she convinced her mother to buy the home in her name. Natasha moved in, determined to build something better for her family. But the unspoken truth lingered in her mind: I've made so much money, but I have nothing to show for it.

A Hard Lesson at Tax Time

At the urging of a friend, Natasha met with a CPA. She walked in confidently, bragging about depositing over $250,000 into her account that year.

Confidence turned into fear the moment the CPA calculated her tax liability.

There were no legitimate deductions.

No proper business structure.

No financial records.

No savings to cover what she owed.

The CPA asked her a question she had avoided for years:

"Where did all the money go?"

Suddenly her glamorous purchases didn't feel like trophies. They felt like evidence.

She listed the expenses out loud.

Car note. Hair. Nails. Clothes. Parties. Trips. Gifts. Clubs.

But the numbers didn't add up.

Natasha had spent hundreds of thousands and had nothing to show for any of it.

A New Chapter Begins

Instead of shaming her, the CPA showed her a way forward. They helped her form an LLC and put structure around a passion she'd always had: healthy cooking. Natasha loved making nutritious meals for her kids, and friends often complimented her dishes.

With guidance, she began selling fresh, prepared meals out of her kitchen. What started as a side hustle turned into a thriving business. Her meals landed in local convenience stores, gyms, and small markets. People loved the taste. They loved the convenience. They loved her.

Eventually, she left the club for good.

Natasha opened multiple locations, created a recognizable brand, and learned what real business felt like: structure, strategy, discipline, and purpose. But even as her business grew, she often replayed her earlier years in her mind.

She didn't regret the past, but she wished she had understood money sooner.

She wished she had saved. She wished she had invested.

She wished she had built a plan before life forced her to.

That wisdom became her fuel, and she used it to build a future she could finally be proud of.

Lessons for Business Owners

1. Fast Money Disappears Fast Without a Plan

Natasha earned more in a weekend than some people earned in a month, but burned through it just as quickly. Wealth requires intention, not impulse.

2. Looks Can Open Doors, but They Don't Build Legacies

Beauty brought Natasha attention, but not stability. A lasting future is built with discipline, structure, and financial strategy, not compliments.

3. Track Income and File Accurate Taxes

Cash-based workers face a high risk of poor record keeping. Natasha could have saved thousands in taxes with proper bookkeeping, business structure, and legitimate deductions.

4. Turn Passion Into Purpose With a Real Business

Her turning point came when she formed an LLC for her meal-prep business. Once she had structure, everything changed: taxes, credibility, and income.

5. Humility Leads to Growth

Natasha's pride in her lifestyle blinded her. The moment she humbled herself and asked for help, her entire life began to change.

6. Think Beyond Today

Natasha never considered what life would look like at forty, fifty, or sixty. Entrepreneurs must create long-term plans that include retirement, investments, insurance, and multiple income streams.

7. Reinvention Is Always Possible

Natasha rebuilt her life in her thirties. You can start at twenty, thirty, forty, or sixty. Progress begins the moment you decide to do better.

Conclusion

Natasha's story is a reminder that money without discipline is a trap. Luxury without strategy is an illusion. Living for attention is the quickest way to lose direction.

She built a second chance by facing hard truths, accepting guidance, and choosing a new path. Every entrepreneur, especially those in cash-based or appearance-driven industries, can learn from her journey.

Because the real glow-up isn't in designer bags or flashy cars.

It's in stability. It's in ownership. It's in building a future you don't have to run from.

Natasha didn't erase her past. She elevated it.

And that's a lesson every business owner can stand on.

Part Three

From Hustler to Businessman: Jason's Journey

Jason had a gift in his hands. From the moment he picked up a pair of clippers in barber school, people noticed. His fades were sharp, his lineups immaculate, and his personality made every client feel like family. Cutting hair wasn't work. It was his art, his passion, and his escape.

After graduating, it didn't take long for Jason's name to ring across the neighborhood. Clients lined up before the shop opened just to get a spot. His chair stayed full, and so did his pockets. Eventually, he saved enough to open his own barbershop. He filled eight stations, charged booth rent, and collected over $2,000 a month from barbers renting chairs.

To everyone watching, Jason had made it.

A young Black man with his own shop, his own team, and his own income. Independent. Respected. Successful. Or so it seemed.

The Shop That Ran Like a Hustle

Jason's shop had a relaxed vibe. Music played. Laughter filled the background. Barbers drifted in and out. As long as booth rent was paid, Jason didn't intervene. There were no employee rules, tracking systems, or set hours. The barbers controlled themselves.

Jason controlled the money coming in, but not where it went.

Whatever he collected often went straight into clothes, shoes, entertainment, or whatever caught his attention that day. He mixed his business income with his personal spending so completely that he couldn't distinguish profit from pocket money.

During tax season, he filed returns full of deductions while reporting very little income. This kept his taxes low. To him, it felt smart. To the IRS, lenders, and banks, it was a financial disaster in the making.

Jason was hustling. He wasn't running a business.

The Woman Who Held Up the Mirror

Then he met someone who changed everything. She was disciplined, business-minded, and successful in her own right. She loved Jason, but she didn't love how loosely he ran his business.

One night, she said gently,

"Baby, you've got something special, but you're not treating it like the business it could be."

Jason brushed it off.

"I am running a business. I have a shop. I pay bills. I make money."

But she challenged him with real questions:

"What was your profit last quarter?"

"What's your overhead?"

"What are your operating expenses?"

"What's your monthly net income after booth rent?"

Jason froze. He had no answers.

For the first time, someone was speaking to him not as a hustler, but as a businessman.

She told him something he would never forget:

"You've got hustle. But you're running a hustle, not a company."

A New Beginning

Jason decided to grow, not only for himself but for her and the future he wanted. She introduced him to her CPA, and that meeting opened his eyes wider than ever before.

With guidance from the CPA, Jason:

- Opened a business bank account
- Installed a POS system to track every dollar
- Stopped mixing personal and business funds
- Began paying himself a salary
- Kept receipts and financial records
- Reviewed financials monthly
- Learned to report taxes accurately

For the first time, Jason could see his business clearly. He understood what was coming in, what was going out, and how much he was truly earning.

With clarity came transformation.

He stopped impulsive spending. He built savings.

He set rules for his barbers.

He treated his shop like the professional establishment it needed to be.

And as the business matured, so did he.

A Man Evolving

Jason's relationship grew stronger, and eventually he married the woman who had pushed him to see his potential. They built businesses together and created a life rooted in discipline, structure, and partnership.

But even in moments of success, Jason reflected:

Why hadn't he learned financial literacy earlier?

Why wasn't it taught in high school?

Why didn't his family understand business well enough to teach him?

Why was generational financial knowledge so limited in his community?

He realized something deeper.

Talent wasn't the problem.

Drive wasn't the problem. Exposure was the issue.

Jason didn't lack skills. He lacked structure. He didn't lack ambition. He lacked education.

That gap had cost him years of growth. But now that he knew better, he did better.

And that made all the difference.

Lessons for Business Owners

1. Separate Business and Personal Money

Jason's entire transformation began when he divided his finances. Business accounts, accounting systems, and payroll are not optional. They are essential.

2. Know Your Numbers

A real business owner understands revenue, expenses, overhead, and profit. If you can't answer basic financial questions about your company, you're operating blindly.

3. Invest in Professional Guidance

Hiring a CPA or financial advisor can change your life. The right expert elevates not only your business, but your mindset.

4. Use Systems, Not Memory

POS systems, bookkeeping software, and digital tracking create accuracy, structure, and growth. Relying on memory is not a business strategy.

5. Financial Education Matters

Jason's story highlights a real issue. Access to financial knowledge is limited in many communities. Entrepreneurs must actively seek education and mentorship.

6. Mindset Is the True Makeover

Jason's skill never changed. His mindset did. Shifting from a hustle mentality to an ownership mentality is the key to lasting success.

7. Strong Relationships Can Elevate You

The right partner or mentor can reveal potential you didn't know you had. Growth happens when you allow others to help you.

Conclusion

Jason's journey is a testament to transformation. He had talent, clients, and a shop, but lacked structure, knowledge, and discipline. Once he embraced proper business practices, everything in his life improved. His income grew. His shop culture strengthened. His opportunities expanded. His family thrived.

His story, like Samantha's and Natasha's, confirms a powerful truth:

Financial literacy is powerful.

Structure is powerful. Discipline is powerful.

Entrepreneurs, especially in underserved communities, are full of potential but often lack the systems that create long-term stability and generational wealth. Jason broke that cycle the moment he chose to learn what no one had taught him growing up.

When he transformed his business, he transformed his life.

Chapter Seven
When Desperation Leads to Disaster

Louis had always been proud of the business he built from the ground up. His small insurance brokerage wasn't flashy, but it was stable. He specialized in auto, trucking, and small-business liability insurance, services few understood well but everyone needed. Over the years, he earned a reputation for honesty, knowledge, and exceptional customer service. His clients trusted him with their livelihoods, and his loyalty to them kept his business consistently profitable.

Louis had no dreams of becoming a billionaire. He simply wanted to grow, hire more staff, upgrade his systems, and secure a stronger financial foundation. He had the experience, the client base, and the ambition.

What he didn't have… was capital.

The Email That Changed Everything

One quiet afternoon, an email landed in Louis' inbox with the subject line:

"New Federal Funding Programs for Small Businesses – Immediate Approval Available."

It looked legitimate. The logo resembled a government seal, the grammar was professional, and the offer seemed promising. It spoke about grants and low-interest loans designed to help small businesses scale and invest in technology.

Everything Louis dreamed of.

Without hesitation, he responded.

A representative quickly scheduled a call. Their tone was polished, the information well-rehearsed, and they requested typical documentation such as tax returns, bank statements, and formation documents. Nothing seemed suspicious. Louis checked every box and submitted everything they requested.

After a week of back-and-forth communication, he received the email he had been praying for:

"Your funding has been approved. Congratulations!"

But there was one condition. He needed to pay a large upfront "release fee" for the funds to be deposited.

They said it was standard. They said it was refundable.

They said he would get it back the same day the funds were released.

Desperate for working capital and excited for the opportunity, Louis wired the payment.

Then he waited. And waited. And waited.

Finally, another message arrived.

"There is an unexpected compliance issue. An additional fee must be paid."

His stomach tightened.

He sent the second payment anyway, hoping this would resolve the issue and keep everything on track.

Days later, the phone number for the representative stopped working.

Emails bounced back. The website disappeared.

It was gone. All of it.

His money. His trust. His stability.

Louis had been scammed.

The Downward Spiral

The timing couldn't have been worse. Louis had already committed to covering the upfront premiums for several large client policies. In his industry, brokers often pay the insurance carriers first, then earn their commission afterward. He expected the funding to support that cash flow.

Now he was on the hook for thousands he didn't have.

Bills piled up. Vendors called daily.

His stress was unbearable.

Desperation pushed him into the next mistake.

The Partner He Never Should Have Chosen

A friend introduced him to a "private investor" who was known for helping struggling business owners. The man dressed well, spoke confidently, and made promises Louis wanted to believe.

He agreed to invest, but only if he became a partner in the business.

Louis, exhausted and drowning financially, agreed without hesitation.

He didn't check references. He didn't verify credentials.

He didn't hire an attorney. He didn't slow down long enough to think.

The partner paid half of the agreed investment upfront and assured Louis the rest was coming soon. He also insisted on hiring someone to "restructure" the company, and although Louis didn't fully understand the need, he agreed. If the partner covered the salary, Louis didn't ask questions.

Within three months, everything fell off.

Operations became chaotic.

The new "restructuring consultant" created confusion instead of order.

The partner became increasingly controlling, showing up unannounced, demanding access to financial systems, and questioning Louis' every decision.

Louis felt like a stranger inside his own business.

The Breaking Point

One morning, after yet another heated disagreement, Louis had a gut feeling that something was seriously wrong. He left the office, drove straight to the bank, and requested to remove the partner's name from all accounts.

But the teller looked at him nervously and said:

"Sir… he's here right now trying to change the access himself."

Louis' heart dropped.

What followed was a long, bitter legal battle. Once attorneys got involved, he learned a painful truth:

The partnership agreement he had signed in desperation granted the partner 50 percent ownership, more than Louis himself intended.

It was legally binding.

And to get out of it, he had to buy the partner out for an amount he didn't have.

Louis ended up borrowing money from his parents just to regain control of the business he originally built alone.

He survived the storm, but his business and spirit were left bruised.

The Hardest Lessons

Louis rebuilt slowly, with caution guiding every step. He became wiser, sharper, and more protective of the business he nearly lost. He learned that desperation clouds judgment, and shortcuts often lead to disaster.

One rushed decision cost him years of progress. But those lessons now guide him and every entrepreneur willing to pay attention.

Lessons for Business Owners

1. **Verify Before You Apply**

   Real government programs never require upfront fees. Louis learned the hard way. Research, verify, and confirm legitimacy before engaging in any funding opportunity.

2. **Vet Every Investor Like They're Hiring You**

   Background checks, references, financial documents, and legal reviews are non-negotiable. If someone wants equity in your business, they must be fully vetted.

3. **Never Sign Without a Lawyer's Eyes**

   Partnership agreements are binding contracts. You must understand every clause, ownership percentage, exit strategy, and liability before signing.

4. **Don't Let Desperation Drive Decisions**

   When emotions are high, judgment is low. Step back, breathe, and consult a professional before making major decisions.

5. **Build Financial Reserves**

   Louis' situation worsened because he had no safety net. Businesses should maintain at least three to six months of operating capital to avoid risky decisions.

6. **Protect Cash Flow in Client Contracts**

   If your business pays upfront costs on behalf of clients, your contracts should protect you:

- deposits
- staggered payments
- late fees
- cancellation terms
- payment due before service

Don't front money without safeguards.

7. **Partnerships Are Like Marriages**

   You must share values, goals, and commitment. Treat partnerships with the long-term seriousness they deserve.

Conclusion

Louis' story is a powerful reminder that opportunity and danger often arrive disguised the same way, especially when you are stressed, overwhelmed, and searching for solutions. His eagerness to expand and his desperation to fix a financial gap opened the door to scammers, manipulators, and a partnership that almost cost him everything.

Yet his story isn't one of defeat. It's one of resilience.

He rebuilt. He learned. He protected what he almost lost.

Entrepreneurs must understand:

Not every opportunity is a blessing. Not every partner is a solution.

Not every problem requires urgent action.

Protect your business with the same intensity you used to build it.

One mistake can destroy years of work, but one decision to slow down, verify, and think strategically can save your future.

Part Two

When Easy Money Turns into a Heavy Burden: Lisa's Story

Lisa was the kind of entrepreneur people admired. She built her consulting firm from nothing, relying on grit, consistency, and a commitment to excellence. Clients trusted her. Her team respected her. Her revenue grew steadily year after year, and for the first time since launching her business, she felt confident enough to think bigger.

Lisa wanted to scale. She wanted to expand her service offerings, strengthen her systems, and position her company for long-term growth. That required capital, and she approached it responsibly. She applied for a business loan, received it, and used it with precision:

- hiring skilled staff
- investing in marketing
- upgrading her infrastructure
- improving client delivery
- It worked.

Her business grew, her profits increased, and she paid the loan off ahead of schedule. That win made her feel unstoppable.

What she didn't know was that this success would soon open a door she wasn't prepared for.

The Flood of Loan Offers

Once the credit bureaus updated her loan payoff, Lisa's inbox started filling with offers from lenders. Some were traditional. Most were alternative lenders, loan companies promising:

- fast approval
- no collateral
- next-day funding
- no credit check

It felt flattering. It felt validating. It felt easy.

And that's where things shifted.

Confident in how well she handled the first loan, Lisa accepted one of the offers. Then another. And another. Before long, she had four active loans, each with its own repayment schedule.

Some of the funds went toward business projects, but truthfully, some didn't. She bought a few personal things she had been wanting, justifying it as a reward for her hard work.

After all, she had managed the first loan with no issue.

Why would these be any different?

But these loans were nothing like the regulated, affordable funding she had handled gracefully before.

When the Payments Start Coming, and They Don't Stop

The new loans came with aggressive repayment terms such as daily and weekly auto-deductions directly from her business account.

At first, it was manageable. Then payroll hit.

Vendors needed payment. A client paid late.

A refund had to be issued. Another lender withdrew their payment.

Then another…

And another…

Soon, Lisa wasn't managing her cash flow, she was juggling it.

She was moving money between accounts. She was delaying payments to cover loan debits.

She was using one loan to float another.

She knew she was in trouble when the money coming in no longer matched the money going out.

And eventually, the worst happened:

Lisa defaulted on one of the loans.

The Legal Storm

The lender didn't wait. They filed suit immediately, freezing a portion of her business account until the matter was resolved. Suddenly:

- she couldn't operate freely
- her team's payroll became difficult
- clients were affected
- attorney fees piled up

All because she accepted loans she didn't need.

Her business, once thriving, was now suffocating under debt she thought she could handle.

The Breaking Point

With no cash reserves left and multiple lenders demanding payment, Lisa did what many business owners fear most:

She filed for bankruptcy.

It was the only way to protect her staff, salvage the core of her business, and start untangling the mess she had created.

In a quiet conversation with a friend, she finally admitted:

"I should have never taken those loans. I didn't need them. Paying off the first loan gave me confidence, but it made me reckless."

Her honesty was painful, but freeing.

Lisa didn't lose her entire business, but she lost valuable time, peace, money, and credibility. And she vowed never to take on unnecessary debt again.

Easy money was not a blessing.

It became a burden.

And it almost cost her everything.

Lessons for Business Owners

1. **Borrow With Purpose, Not Emotion**

   Lisa borrowed because she could, not because she needed to. Funding should always support a clear, measurable purpose, not a moment of excitement or convenience.

2. **Understand Every Loan Term Clearly**

Quick loans often come with aggressive repayment structures, daily or weekly drafts that strangle cash flow. Always calculate how repayments will impact your monthly operations before signing.

3. **Keep Business Funds and Personal Expenses Separate**

   Using business loans for personal spending creates chaos, financially and tax-wise. Keep business money for business and personal money for personal use.

4. **Don't Stack Loans or Overleverage**

   Multiple loans create an impossible cycle. Just because someone offers you credit doesn't mean you should take it. Debt should be strategic, not a fallback plan.

5. **Prioritize Cash Flow Management**

   Before adding new obligations, assess:

   - your slow months
   - current liabilities
   - upcoming expenses
   - your financial buffer

Cash flow, not profit, is the lifeline of every business.

6. **Get Professional Advice Before Borrowing**

   A CPA or financial advisor can prevent costly mistakes. One consultation could have stopped Lisa from taking any of the four loans she didn't need.

7. **Mistakes Happen, Rebuilding Is Possible**

   Lisa took accountability. Bankruptcy wasn't the ending, it was a reset. Every entrepreneur will make a financial decision they regret. What matters most is learning and rebuilding.

Conclusion

Lisa's story is a powerful reminder that easy money always comes with strings attached. Her ambition wasn't the problem. Her lack of restraint and planning was. Loans are tools, not lifelines, and when misused, they tighten around a business until the owner can't breathe.

Just like Louis, Lisa discovered that not all money is good money.

Some opportunities look helpful but lead to financial disaster.

The most valuable capital a business owner can have isn't borrowed. It's:

- financial discipline
- strategic planning
- professional guidance
- the wisdom to say no, even when yes looks tempting

Her journey teaches us that access to money without a plan is a trap, and financial responsibility is what truly protects and sustains a business.

Part Three

When Smart Boundaries Save Your Business: Izabella's Story

Izabella was a rising star in the beauty industry. Her lash extensions and brow-sculpting services had earned her a devoted clientele that booked months in advance. Her studio was clean, classy, and always buzzing. She had built her brand from scratch, one perfectly shaped brow at a time.

Beyond her hands-on work, Izabella expanded her impact by hosting workshops and seminars that attracted both new and experienced beauty professionals. Her classes sold out regularly, generating another reliable stream of revenue. Her business was growing, and more importantly, it was stable.

So when a longtime friend, also in the beauty industry, approached her with a partnership idea, it seemed like a natural next step. They respected one another, moved in similar circles, and shared the same passion for beauty and education. Combining their strengths felt like an opportunity to reach new heights.

Izabella was open to the idea, but she wasn't naive.

She insisted on one critical boundary:

Her original business, brand, assets, client list, and intellectual property would remain legally separate.

They would form a new company together, but Izabella's existing business would remain hers alone. Her attorney drafted a clear agreement outlining ownership, responsibilities, and protections. With that safeguard in place, she confidently moved forward.

A Partnership That Started Strong

For the first year and a half, the partnership blossomed. They offered specialized beauty services through the new company, collaborated on classes, and shared clients. The joint venture gained traction and their combined following grew.

But success began to expose differences.

Izabella noticed her partner's commitment fading.

Invoices were left unpaid. Responsibilities were ignored.

Meetings were missed. Communication became strained.

Izabella tried to address the issues, but her partner brushed off the concerns or made excuses. What started as minor irritation became a growing red flag.

The Breaking Point

Finally, Izabella scheduled a formal meeting to discuss the problems. She hoped they could realign, adjust responsibilities, or agree on a new direction.

Instead, the conversation exploded.

Her partner accused her of "trying to control everything" and claimed ownership rights over the joint business, as well as her original company. Things escalated quickly. Veiled threats turned into open hostility.

Within days, Izabella was served with a lawsuit.

Her former friend was now demanding ownership of a business she never built and attempting to pull Izabella's personal brand into the legal mess.

What Saved Izabella

The lawsuit was stressful, expensive, and emotionally draining. Losing a business partner was one thing; losing a friend was another. But Izabella knew she had done one thing right from the very beginning:

She protected her foundation.

Her original business, trademarks, content, and financial accounts were legally separate from the partnership. The contracts were airtight. When the case went before the court, every boundary she established held up.

The judge dissolved the partnership and upheld the agreement:

- Izabella kept her original business, untouched.
- She retained 100 percent of her brand.
- She walked away with her reputation and assets intact.

Her partner walked away empty-handed.

The experience scared her, but it didn't break her. Instead, it reminded her of something powerful:

Your business can survive a storm when the foundation is strong.

Izabella rebuilt her peace, strengthened her boundaries, and returned to her studio more protective, more focused, and wiser than before.

Lessons for Business Owners

1. **Always Legally Separate Your Business Entities**

   Izabella's saving grace was keeping her original company separate from the new partnership. Never attach your entire livelihood to a joint venture.

2. **Get an Attorney-Prepared Partnership Agreement**

   Friendship is not protection. Legal contracts are. Document everything clearly before entering a partnership of any kind.

3. **Protect Your Brand and Intellectual Property**

   Your logo, courses, content, systems, and client list are valuable assets. Secure them through trademarks, copyrights, and contractual separation.

4. **Address Issues Early. Don't Let Them Slide**

   Early accountability can prevent major conflicts. Red flags do not disappear; they grow.

5. **Personal Relationships Don't Replace Professional Safeguards**

   People change. Emotions shift. Money exposes character. Treat all partnerships as business decisions.

6. **Hope for the Best but Plan for the Worst**

   Exit clauses, ownership definitions, and legal structures exist for protection. Use them.

7. **Move Forward Smarter, Not Bitter**

Izabella didn't allow betrayal to stop her. She used the experience to strengthen her standards and her business.

Conclusion: The Price of Unprotected Decisions

The stories of Louis, Lisa, and Izabella reveal different sides of entrepreneurship, but they all point to one universal truth:

Success doesn't just depend on what you build, it depends on how well you protect it.

Louis' downfall began with trust placed in the wrong opportunity and the wrong partner.

Lisa's unraveling started with borrowing money she didn't need and couldn't sustain.

Izabella's survival came from planning ahead, even when things felt safe.

Their journeys highlight critical realities every business owner must understand:

- Desperation leads to dangerous decisions.
- Easy money becomes expensive debt.
- Friendships do not guarantee good business partnerships.
- Legal and financial protection matter just as much as strategy and skill.
- Your future depends on the decisions you make today.

Louis shows us how scams and rushed partnerships can destroy years of work.

Lisa shows how overleveraging can suffocate even a profitable business.

Izabella shows how preparation prevents destruction.

Together, their stories deliver a clear message:

Don't move based on emotion.

Don't borrow based on impulse.

Don't partner based on trust alone.

Operate with vision, discipline, and vigilance.

Because the real power in entrepreneurship isn't just the ability to grow,

it's the ability to protect what you have grown.

A business without boundaries is vulnerable. A business without structure is unstable.

A business without protection is one crisis away from collapse.

But a business built with wisdom, strategy, and strong legal foundations?

That business lasts. These stories are not warnings. They are blueprints.

Blueprints for building a business that doesn't just make money…but stands the test of time.

Chapter 8
The Danger of Poor Leadership

Sharon had built her call center from the ground up, brick by brick. It took five long years of sacrifice, long nights, and missed holidays before she began seeing real profits. She had a team of 20 employees who respected her not just as their boss, but as a leader. Sharon cultivated a culture of encouragement, collaboration, and trust. She praised her team regularly, celebrated their achievements with incentives and small gifts, and valued their input by implementing their ideas. Her leadership created a thriving and motivated workplace.

Eventually, Sharon reached a point where she wanted to step back and enjoy the fruits of her labor. She needed someone to help her manage daily operations so she could focus on other opportunities. After an exhaustive hiring process, she brought in a manager who appeared to be a perfect fit. She had a bachelor's degree in management, a clean background, and glowing references. Sharon trained her personally for a few weeks, showing her the systems, expectations, and the culture she worked so hard to build. Confident in her new hire, Sharon began stepping back from day-to-day operations.

Within a few weeks, one of Sharon's top-performing employees resigned without warning. When Sharon asked around, the other team members casually mentioned that the employee found another job. A little puzzled, Sharon didn't dig deeper at the time. But then, another high-performing employee submitted her two weeks' notice. This time, Sharon personally spoke with her, offering a raise and other incentives to stay. The employee respectfully declined with no detailed explanation.

Sharon's concern grew. She began visiting the office more frequently and engaging with her staff. One day, she quietly observed the manager interacting with the team. What she witnessed shocked her. The manager was yelling at employees, harshly criticizing their performance, and creating a tense and fear-driven environment. Sharon confronted her immediately, making it clear that this behavior was unacceptable and had to stop.

For a short while, things seemed to improve. Sharon resumed her reduced schedule, believing the manager had taken her warnings seriously. However, at the end of the quarter, the company's numbers told a different story. Revenue had declined significantly, especially in the call center division. Sharon asked her accountant to analyze the losses, and the data confirmed what she feared. The decline in profits was directly linked to the call center's performance.

Determined to find the root cause, Sharon conducted private one-on-one meetings with her employees. Most said things were "fine" and avoided offering any real insight. It wasn't until she spoke with her most senior team members that the truth came out. The employee admitted the manager regularly yelled, micromanaged, belittled them during meetings, and humiliated team members by playing back calls and mocking their performance in front of others.

Sharon was stunned and heartbroken. She felt betrayed, not only by the manager but by the silence of her team. Wanting to confirm this behavior with her own eyes, Sharon devised a plan. She told the manager she'd be out of town for several weeks, then returned quietly through the back entrance one morning. Sure enough, she overheard the manager berating an employee, calling her "stupid" and threatening to send her home for not closing sales.

After listening in disbelief for 20 minutes, Sharon stepped in. The manager defensively explained that the employee wasn't following directions. But Sharon had heard enough. She terminated her on the spot.

It took Sharon nearly two full quarters to rebuild morale and repair the damage to her team culture. She had to regain the trust of her employees, reassure them of the company's values, and most importantly, step back into the leadership role that made her business successful in the first place.

Solutions and Lessons Learned

1. **Never Fully Detach from Leadership**

   Even with strong systems in place, business owners should remain involved at some level. Delegating authority does not mean disengaging. Regular check-ins, staff meetings, and monitoring culture are vital to staying informed.

2. **Culture is Fragile, Protect It**

   A toxic leader can undo years of positive culture in a matter of weeks. When hiring managers, don't just assess their credentials. Assess their emotional intelligence and interpersonal style. Culture fit is more important than a perfect resume.

3. **Create Safe Channels for Feedback**

   Employees may be hesitant to speak up about problems, especially if they fear retaliation. Implement anonymous surveys or regular confidential one-on-one sessions that allow team members to voice concerns safely.

4. **Observe Before Reacting**

   Sharon's undercover observation gave her undeniable evidence. Sometimes leaders must investigate discreetly to uncover the real issues. This allowed her to act decisively and justifiably.

5. **Document Employee Morale and Performance Trends**

   Regularly track turnover, sales trends, and employee satisfaction. Sudden changes may indicate deeper issues, as they did in Sharon's case. Don't ignore early warning signs.

6. **Reinforce Core Values with New Hires**

   Make your company values non-negotiable. Train all new hires, including managers, on not just the processes but also the expected tone, behavior, and leadership style that aligns with your company culture.

7. **Recovering from Toxic Leadership Takes Time**

   Be patient and intentional when rebuilding after a toxic manager. Focus on team-building activities, transparent communication, and re-establishing trust.

8. **Trust, but Verify**

   Even with good references, always follow up with ongoing performance evaluations. Someone may be great on paper but ineffective, or even harmful, in your specific environment.

Final Thought

Great leaders don't just build businesses, they build people. Delegation is necessary for growth, but leadership should never be fully outsourced. Protecting your team's culture is not a luxury, it's a leadership duty.

The Pitfalls of Poor Delegation

Siemon was the definition of a serial entrepreneur. Ambitious, driven, and always on the move, he had multiple businesses running simultaneously, from retail to consulting and even a few investment properties. With so much on his plate, Siemon often found himself burned out, only to recover briefly and throw himself back into the hustle. Personal time was nonexistent, and the mounting pressure made it clear: he needed help.

After some thought, Siemon hired a personal assistant, a seemingly perfect solution. The assistant was sharp, eager, and ready to relieve Siemon of his non-essential tasks. On the first day, Siemon handed him a detailed list of responsibilities: managing all calls, handling appointments, monitoring emails, organizing files, handling dry cleaning, and coordinating all personal errands. Siemon gave a quick tour of the office, showed him where things were, and moved on, grateful to finally have some breathing room.

For the next six months, Siemon fully leaned on his new assistant. He stopped checking emails. Calls were missed. He rarely came to the office. Whenever anyone needed something, he simply said, "Talk to my assistant."

But when Siemon eventually returned to the office, he was hit with a wave of disappointment. Documents were disorganized, tasks had been forgotten, and multiple issues had been left unresolved. Frustrated, Siemon confronted the assistant, listing everything that had gone wrong. He demanded to know why the assistant had failed to complete the tasks that had been assigned.

The assistant remained calm and respectful, listening to Siemon vent. When Siemon finally asked, "Why wasn't it done?" the assistant replied plainly:

"I'm not a mind reader. You gave me a list, but no instructions on how you wanted things done. Some of the tasks I completed using my best judgment, but I'm not sure if they meet your standards. You never showed me your filing system. You never told me what questions to ask clients. I've been making appointments blindly without knowing what services you offer in detail. I've done my best, but I've been left to figure everything out alone."

Siemon was taken aback. He hadn't realized how little guidance he had provided. The assistant wasn't lazy or incompetent; he was untrained. Siemon apologized on the spot, acknowledging his failure to properly onboard someone into a role that touched so many critical parts of his business. He committed to spending the next week with his assistant, walking him through processes, answering questions, clarifying expectations, and building a structure to ensure success.

Solutions and Lessons Learned

1. **Delegation Without Direction Leads to Disappointment**

   Simply assigning tasks is not the same as training someone to handle them correctly. Clear instructions, expectations, and context are essential for successful delegation.

2. **Create a Standard Operating Procedure (SOP)**

   Every recurring task should have a written guide. SOPs save time, reduce errors, and provide a consistent reference for assistants or future hires.

3. **Conduct a Formal Onboarding Process**

   Even for an assistant, proper onboarding is critical. Take time to explain tools, communication protocols, organizational systems, and your leadership style.

4. **Don't Assume Competence Equals Clarity**

A skilled assistant is still new to your systems. Even the most talented professional needs context to thrive in a new environment.

5. **Check In Regularly**

   Especially in the early stages, schedule weekly or biweekly check-ins to answer questions, review progress, and fine-tune tasks. Delegation is not "set it and forget it."

6. **Empower With Information**

   Give your assistant access to client intake forms, FAQ sheets, internal workflows, and anything else that helps them make informed decisions on your behalf.

7. **Clarify Communication Preferences**

   If you want your calendar managed in a certain way or emails categorized by urgency, communicate that. The assistant can only mirror what's clearly stated.

8. **Recognize and Own Leadership Gaps**

   Siemon's willingness to accept his own oversight and take corrective action saved the working relationship and ultimately improved his business operations.

Final Thought

Delegation is not just about removing tasks from your plate. It's about transferring responsibility with clarity. Great leaders don't just assign work, they empower their team with the tools, knowledge, and support needed to execute with excellence.

The Risk of Over-Reliance on One Employee

Mike owned a growing and respected IT services company. With a specialized clientele of mid-sized to large corporations, many with over 200 employees, his company provided support for technical infrastructure, software integrations, and on-site troubleshooting. His team was small but mighty, consisting of six capable staff members who were skilled and responsive.

Due to the nature of their business, work hours weren't standard 9 to 5. Clients needed immediate responses when systems went down, and Mike's team often had to jump into action quickly, whether remotely or in person. Amid this fast-paced environment, there was one standout employee, let's call him Jordan. Jordan had a unique ability to troubleshoot issues with precision, build strong rapport with clients, and handle pressure with professionalism.

Because of his exceptional skills, Mike leaned on Jordan more than anyone else. He trusted him with the most complex clients and most critical emergencies. But as the dependency grew, so did the imbalance.

Whenever Jordan requested time off, Mike approved it, but often with a catch. He'd remind him to "bring your laptop just in case," and almost without fail, a so-called "emergency" would arise that pulled Jordan away from his vacation. Whether on a beach with his family or taking a few personal days, Jordan was repeatedly contacted to handle high-priority issues. Over time, he grew frustrated and exhausted. He quietly vented to co-workers about being overworked and underappreciated, but he never brought it directly to Mike.

One afternoon, while chatting with another employee in the break room, Mike overheard something that caught his attention. The team member mentioned how Jordan felt overworked and how unfair the treatment seemed compared to others on the team.

Curious and a little concerned, Mike asked for more details. The employee elaborated, confirming what Mike hadn't fully realized.

That evening, Mike shared the situation with his wife. She asked him bluntly:

"Is it true that he's always working during vacations?"

"Do you rely on him more than the others?"

"Do you think that's fair?"

"Are you compensating him correctly for the extra weight he carries?"

Those questions hit Mike hard. He started to reflect on how often Jordan had sacrificed his personal time and how little recognition he had received in return.

A few days later, Mike called Jordan into his office. He was honest and direct.

"I heard that you may be feeling burnt out and mistreated. Is that true?"

Jordan looked at him and said:

"Yes. I love my job, and I'm proud of what I do, but I'm tired. I carry the heaviest load, and every vacation turns into a remote work session. I just want to feel like I'm valued and not the go-to emergency guy every time something breaks."

Mike listened. Really listened. Then he decided.

He offered Jordan a promotion, elevating him to a leadership position with partial equity in the company, recognizing not just his work ethic but his value to the company's growth. He also guaranteed two full weeks of uninterrupted vacation time each year. No calls. No laptop. Just rest.

Jordan was thrilled. His energy and loyalty were renewed. Not only did he stay, but his new leadership role helped Mike scale the business even further, creating structure, better delegation, and greater employee satisfaction across the board.

Solutions and Lessons Learned

1. **Over-Reliance on One Employee Creates Burnout and Resentment**

   When one person carries more weight than the rest without proper support, it leads to fatigue, frustration, and eventual disengagement. Balance responsibilities among your team and train backups for key roles.

2. **Recognize and Reward Above-and-Beyond Contributions**

   Employees who consistently go the extra mile should be rewarded not just with praise, but with promotions, bonuses, or even equity when appropriate. Recognition is not optional, it's essential.

3. **Respect Time Off Fully**

   Vacations are meant to be restorative. Contacting employees during their time off defeats the purpose and can lead to burnout. Create systems that allow people to truly unplug.

4. **Listen to Quiet Frustrations**

Not every concern will be voiced directly. Pay attention to what employees say to each other or mention in passing. These insights can reveal critical issues before they escalate.

5. **Have Honest Conversations About Expectations**

   Mike's conversation with Jordan was a turning point. Regular one-on-one check-ins provide a safe space for employees to share how they're really doing, mentally, emotionally, and professionally.

6. **Don't Confuse Dependability with Indestructibility**

   Just because someone is capable and committed doesn't mean they can handle unlimited stress. High performers need boundaries too.

7. **Build a Succession Plan for Every Role**

   Avoid bottlenecks by cross-training your team. Every role, especially a mission-critical one, should have at least one backup to ensure business continuity without overwhelming a single individual.

8. **Leadership Requires Self-Reflection**

   Mike's growth as a leader came through reflection and feedback. Great leaders are willing to ask themselves tough questions and course-correct when necessary.

Final Thought

When you build a company around one rockstar employee, you don't build a team; you build dependency. Empowerment, fairness, and proper support systems are the cornerstones of a sustainable and successful business.

Conclusion: Leadership Blind Spots and the Cost of Delegation Done Wrong

The stories of Sharon, Siemon, and Mike are strikingly different in industry and structure, but each reveals a common thread that haunts many entrepreneurs: the unintended consequences of mismanaging leadership, delegation, and employee well-being.

Sharon's story shows us what happens when a leader steps away without safeguarding the culture that made their business thrive. Her attempt to delegate leadership to a qualified manager without maintaining oversight resulted in a toxic environment, the loss of key employees, and declining performance. It served as a powerful reminder that delegation without accountability can become a slow leak that drains both morale and revenue.

Siemon's journey highlighted another common pitfall, assuming that handing off a task is enough. Delegation without instruction is just as damaging as no delegation at all. His assistant didn't fail; he was set up to operate in the dark. Once Siemon realized that successful delegation requires systems, support, and clarity, he was able to turn things around and build a more effective working relationship.

Mike's experience teaches us about the dangers of over-reliance. By leaning too heavily on one high-performing employee, he created an unbalanced and unfair workplace dynamic. What started as admiration for excellence turned into exploitation, unintended but impactful. His ability to reflect, acknowledge the issue, and elevate his employees helped transform not only their relationship but the entire direction of his company.

Key Takeaways

1. **Delegation is a Skill, not a Shortcut**

   Giving someone a task doesn't guarantee success. Without clear expectations, guidance, and support, delegation fails and so does leadership.

2. **Leadership Requires Constant Presence and Awareness**

   Even when stepping back, leaders must remain connected to culture, performance, and the well-being of their teams.

3. **Feedback, Both Given and Received, Is Invaluable**

   Encourage a culture where employees feel safe sharing concerns. Listen actively and act decisively when needed.

4. **Recognize and Respect the Human Side of Business**

   Behind every role is a person with limits, needs, and aspirations. Whether it's time off, recognition, or boundaries, leaders must remember that sustainability matters for everyone.

5. **The Best Leaders Stay Teachable**

   Whether the lesson comes from an employee's comment, a failed system, or a spouse's insight, staying open to growth is the mark of true leadership.

In the end, business success isn't just about profit margins or scaling operations. It's about people. And when leaders neglect the human element, even the most promising business can begin to falter. Chapter 8 reminds us that leadership is not about doing everything. It's about doing the right things, with the right people, in the right way.

Chapter 9: When Hustle Becomes Harmful – The High Cost of Neglecting Self-Care

Sandra was a powerhouse dedicated entrepreneur who built her business from the ground up. She was the definition of "hands-on," involved in every detail of the company's day-to-day operations. From answering every client's email to handling late-night requests, Sandra poured every ounce of her energy into the success of her business. Work didn't stop on weekends or holidays. If a client had an issue, Sandra was on no matter the time or place.

Her inbox was always spotless, her calendar packed, and her focus unshakable. But what looked like dedication on the outside was slowly becoming self-destruction on the inside.

Sandra had a competent office manager who repeatedly warned her:

"You're building bad habits. You need to take care of yourself. The business can't run if you run yourself into the ground."

But Sandra brushed it off. She believed her clients needed her and that taking time off would somehow harm the business. She wore her burnout like a badge of honor.

Then one day, everything stopped.

While working at the office, Sandra suddenly felt sharp chest pains. Alarmed, her team rushed her to the hospital, fearing a heart attack. After extensive tests, the doctors delivered a diagnosis

Sandra wasn't expecting: extreme stress. No heart damage yet, but her body was waving a red flag.

"You need to slow down," they told her. "This isn't sustainable."

Sandra returned to work and considered the doctor's words, but she didn't change much. The cycle resumed.

Emails. Calls. Weekend availability.

She still placed the business above everything, her family, her health, and her peace of mind.

Three months later, it happened again. Another episode, this time more serious. She was hospitalized for four days. This time, the doctors were clear:

"If you don't make lifestyle changes, your body will give out. Stress can and will kill you."

This time, the message stuck.

When Sandra returned to work, the leadership team scheduled a staff meeting. The manager, who had watched Sandra burn herself out for years, spoke up candidly:

"You taught your clients that your time has no value. You set no boundaries. You taught them that you'd be available 24/7. You gave them not only your services but yourself."

"You became their therapist, their friend, their lifeline. And while your heart was in the right place, you forgot something important: you can't pour from an empty cup."

The team rallied behind her. Together, they created a new plan:

• They hired additional staff to absorb some of Sandra's workload.

• They restricted Sandra's availability and gave her designated office days.

• Two full days each week were blocked off as non-working days, no calls, no emails.

• They helped her reframe how she showed up as a leader, no longer as the do-it-all problem solver, but as the visionary, the strategist, and most importantly, the human.

Solutions and Lessons Learned

1. **Entrepreneurship Shouldn't Cost You Your Health**

   Running a business is demanding, but it should never be at the expense of your physical or mental well-being. Health is not a luxury, it's a requirement to lead effectively.

2. **Burnout is Not a Badge of Honor**

   Many entrepreneurs confuse hustle with heroism. Working around the clock may feel productive, but it's a path to collapse. Sustainable success requires rest.

3. **Train Your Clients How to Treat You**

   When you respond to emails at midnight and take calls on weekends, you teach your clients to expect constant access. Boundaries don't harm service, they preserve it.

4. **Separate Your Service from Your Self-Worth**

Your business may be personal to you, but you are not your business. Clients are paying for a service, not you. Learn to separate emotional attachment from professional delivery.

5. **Build Systems That Don't Depend on You Alone**

   Hiring, training, and building systems that function without your constant presence is a sign of strong leadership, not detachment. Trust your team. Empower them to carry the load.

6. **Your Business Can Survive Without You, But You Can't Without Rest**

   No amount of income, recognition, or growth is worth your life. If your business can't operate without you being available 24/7, it's time to rethink the model.

7. **Balance Must Be Built Intentionally**

   Sandra's solution came from structured changes: adjusted schedules, boundaries, and team support. Balance doesn't just happen, it's built through deliberate choices and reinforced daily.

8. **Heed the Warning Signs the First Time**

   Sandra's first hospital visit was the warning. The second one was the consequence. Don't wait for a major breakdown to make the necessary life and business changes.

Final Thought

You are your business's greatest asset, but you're also a person first. You deserve to live a life that includes rest, joy, and personal fulfillment. The business will grow, evolve, and thrive, but only if you do too.

Trusting the Team and Taking Time to Heal

Tom was the kind of business owner who believed that hard work could fix anything. He was ambitious, driven, and constantly chasing the next opportunity. While his primary business kept him busy enough, he regularly partnered in other ventures, eager to expand his reach and his income. He was the last one to leave the office most nights, and sometimes, he didn't leave at all.

Tom's wife, patient but increasingly frustrated, tried to get him to slow down. They came up with compromises: scheduled date nights, dedicated family dinners, weekends without work. But even when Tom was physically present, his mind was still in business thinking, planning, and responding to messages. Though well-intentioned, the balance they hoped for never truly materialized.

Then tragedy struck. First, Tom lost his brother, a devastating blow that shook him to his core. Before he could fully process that loss, he lost his father as well. These back-to-back tragedies sent Tom into a quiet emotional spiral. Rather than confront the pain, he buried himself deeper in work.

He stopped sleeping well. His appetite was inconsistent. He started having heart palpitations and a constant sense of anxiety he couldn't shake. He felt like he was holding the entire world together, and it was starting to crack beneath his feet.

His wife, recognizing the toll it was taking on him, insisted he see a doctor. After a full evaluation, the diagnosis was clear: stress and unresolved grief. The doctor warned that if Tom didn't take time to process his emotions and get rest, his physical and mental health would continue to decline.

With his wife's help and support, Tom stepped back. She temporarily took over managing the business operations and gave him the space to heal. During this time, he focused on rest, therapy, and mourning the losses he had tried to avoid. It was uncomfortable, but necessary.

When Tom returned to work weeks later, he expected to find a mess. But instead, he found stability. His staff had stepped up. The systems he had built were working. Projects were on track, deadlines had been met, and nothing had fallen apart.

That moment was eye-opening. For the first time, Tom realized the truth:

It wasn't that he couldn't take time away. It was that he didn't trust that he could.

He finally saw what his team was capable of. The support was there all along, he had just never let it work without him.

Solutions and Lessons Learned

1. **Grief Demands Attention, Not Avoidance**

   Avoiding emotional pain by burying yourself in work doesn't resolve it, it delays healing and multiplies stress. Give yourself permission to grieve and seek help when you need it.

2. **Health Will Force What You Refuse to Prioritize**

   Tom ignored the signs until his body made it impossible. Stress, insomnia, and heart issues are not just symptoms, they are signals. Address them early.

3. **Don't Underestimate Your Team**

   Many business owners operate with the false belief that only they can keep things running. But a well-trained team with clear systems can often do more than you think if you allow them to.

4. **Trust Is a Leadership Skill**

   Micromanagement often stems from fear. Learning to trust your team is just as important as hiring the right people. Delegate with confidence, not hesitation.

5. **Temporary Absence Is Not Abandonment**

   Stepping away for your mental health, grief, or personal recovery doesn't mean you're abandoning your business. It means you're ensuring you'll be strong enough to continue leading it.

6. **Let Others Help**

   Tom's wife played a key role in holding things together during his recovery. Don't be afraid to lean on loved ones, team members, or professionals. Leadership doesn't mean doing it alone.

7. **Build Resilient Systems**

   Business continuity shouldn't rely on one person. Invest time in creating processes, cross-training staff, and establishing communication protocols that allow the business to operate smoothly even in your absence.

8. **Balance Isn't Just for Avoiding Burnout, It's for Surviving Life**

   Life will happen. Illness, loss, and setbacks are inevitable. Creating balance and flexibility in your business allows you to step away when you need to and return without fear.

Final Thought

Tom's story is a powerful reminder that even the strongest leaders can't outrun grief, and that building a business isn't just about money, it's about building support. Real success includes the ability to take a break, to heal, and to trust the systems and people you've put in place. You don't have to carry it all alone, and you were never meant to.

When It's Too Late to Rest

Mary was the definition of a high-achieving entrepreneur. Over the course of two decades, she built multiple successful businesses, each one a reflection of her relentless drive, long hours, and unwavering commitment to excellence. She was well-known in her industry, respected by peers, and financially secure. But all of it came at a cost.

While Mary's career flourished, her personal life was strained. She had a husband and children, but she rarely spent meaningful time with them. Family dinners were often missed. School events were sacrificed for meetings. Her husband became the primary caregiver, managing the children's lives and maintaining the household while Mary focused on scaling her businesses.

The disconnect began to show in their marriage. Over time, resentment built up. Her husband, exhausted and emotionally distant, gave her an ultimatum:

"Come with us on a family vacation, disconnect from work, and learn how to enjoy life again or we may not survive this marriage."

Mary didn't want to lose her family. So, for the first time in years, she stepped away. They traveled out of the country for a two-week family trip. And something unexpected happened, she experienced joy.

Uninterrupted, device-free, soul-filling joy.

She laughed. She reconnected. She rested.

For the first time in decades, Mary realized what she had been missing. And when the plane landed back home, she cried.

From that point forward, Mary committed to putting her family first. They planned monthly adventure movie nights, road trips, simple moments that brought them together again. Six months passed. The bond that had frayed was healing. Life finally felt full, not just successful.

One weekend, they went hiking as a family. It was beautiful sunlight streaming through the trees, laughter echoing through the trail. Her husband was walking ahead, joking with the kids. But suddenly, he realized he hadn't heard Mary's voice behind him.

He turned around and saw her collapsing on the ground.

Panicked, he ran to her side, screaming for help. But by the time the paramedics arrived, it was too late. Mary had died of a heart attack on the trail.

Her family was devastated. Her husband, heartbroken, sat in disbelief.

For twenty years, she had pushed herself to the limit. And just when she was finally learning how to rest, reconnect, and reclaim her life, she was gone.

Solutions and Lessons Learned

1. **Rest Is Not a Reward, It's a Right**

   Mary waited too long to take a break. We often treat rest like something we "earn," but rest is essential to survival. The body and mind can only go so long before they break down.

2. **No Amount of Success Can Replace Presence**

   Mary had built empires but missed the very moments that mattered most. Business growth means little if it comes at the expense of family memories and emotional connection.

3. **Listen to the Warnings Before It's Too Late**

   Whether it's burnout, physical symptoms, or loved ones expressing concern, listen. The signs are there. Don't wait for a crisis to finally act.

4. **There's No Such Thing as "Catching Up Later" with Family**

   Mary believed there would always be more time. But moments with loved ones aren't guaranteed. Investing in relationships now is more valuable than any future or paycheck.

5. **Redefine the Meaning of Success**

   True success isn't just found in profit margins, brand growth, or public recognition. It's found in laughter around the dinner table, peace in your body, and joy in your life.

6. **Make Self-Care a Non-Negotiable**

Schedule rest. Prioritize health checkups. Know your limits. Build your business around your life, not the other way around.

7. **Build a Life, Not Just a Legacy**

   Mary left behind a powerful legacy, but she didn't get to fully live the life she worked so hard to create. Balance your pursuit of legacy with the beauty of being fully alive in the present.

Final Thought

Mary's story is a haunting but powerful reminder that tomorrow is never promised. As entrepreneurs, we often sacrifice today for a better "someday," but what if someday never comes?

Take the trip. Hold your family tight. Sleep in. Laugh loud.

Because success without life isn't success at all, it's just survival in disguise.

The Silent Toll of Neglecting Self-Care

Sandra, Tom, and Mary each built their businesses with grit, ambition, and relentless commitment. They were powerful examples of what determination can achieve, but also solemn reminders of what it can cost.

Sandra ignored the early warning signs of burnout until her body demanded rest. Tom buried his grief in his work until it manifested as physical and emotional collapse. Mary devoted decades to success, only realizing what truly mattered when it was nearly too late, and tragically, it was.

These stories carry one unified message: your business will only be as healthy as you are.

Entrepreneurs often wear overwork like a badge of honor, believing rest is a luxury, balance is weakness, and availability equals value. But that mindset is a silent killer, not just of health, but of relationships, joy, and peace of mind. True leadership isn't about how much you do, it's about how well you build, how wisely you lead, and how intentionally you live.

Each of these individuals had the means to rest, the people to support them, and the ability to set boundaries. What they lacked was permission from themselves.

Unified Lessons from Chapter 9

- Success without self-care is short-lived. If your business thrives but your health deteriorates, the cost is too high.
- You're not irreplaceable, but you are invaluable. Letting go doesn't mean losing control. It means trusting your systems and your team.
- Time is your most precious asset. You can rebuild a business. You can't relive missed moments with your family or recover years of lost peace.
- Balance is not a sign of laziness, it's a sign of maturity. You can be ambitious and rested, driven and present, powerful and human.

Final Reflection

Your business is an extension of your vision, but it's not your entire identity. Sandra got a second chance, Tom learned to trust his team, but Mary's story reminds us that time doesn't wait for anyone. Don't wait for a crisis to prioritize your life. Redefine success now, not just in revenue, but in rest, relationships, and joy.

Because you are the heart of your business.

And if the heart stops, so does everything else.

Chapter 10
When Verbal Agreements Turn into Legal Nightmares

The Story: Frank's Informal Partnership

Frank had always wanted to be a business owner. So when the opportunity arose to start a small logistics company, he jumped at it with both feet. He had the industry knowledge, the work ethic, and the vision—but not quite enough startup capital. That gap was filled by his close friend, Marcus.

Marcus had a stable 9-to-5 job and disposable income, but no desire to run a business. He offered to provide the startup funds under one clear condition: **he would be a silent partner**.

A silent partner—by definition—is an investor who contributes capital but does not participate in daily operations, decision-making, or management. They do not hire staff, negotiate contracts, manage customers, or control bank accounts. Their role is passive. In exchange for staying silent, they typically receive a defined return on investment or a percentage of profits, while the operating partner assumes the risk, responsibility, and workload.

That was exactly the understanding Frank believed they shared.

Their verbal agreement was simple: Marcus would front the startup capital, Frank would build and run the business entirely, Marcus would be repaid within two years, and profits would be split 60/40 in Frank's favor. No lawyers. No paperwork. Just trust between friends.

From day one, Frank carried the weight of the business alone.

He secured clients, negotiated contracts, managed drivers, handled compliance, oversaw billing, and solved problems at all hours of the day. He worked long days and sacrificed personal time, often reinvesting profits back into the company to keep it growing. Marcus, meanwhile, remained completely hands-off—no meetings, no decisions, no involvement—exactly as a silent partner is supposed to be.

Within a year, the company was thriving.

True to his word, Frank began repaying Marcus in structured installments. The business was profitable, visible, and gaining momentum. That's when the dynamic shifted.

As revenue increased, Marcus's silence began to fade.

He started asking for detailed financial reports. Then he questioned operational decisions. Soon after, he expressed interest in being involved in day-to-day activities—despite having built none of the systems, relationships, or infrastructure that made the business successful.

Frank was blindsided.

He reminded Marcus of their original understanding: Marcus was a silent partner. Frank had built the business from the ground up—alone. But Marcus's position had changed. He now claimed that because he provided the initial capital, he was entitled to more authority, more involvement, and eventually, equal control.

What started as casual questions turned into pressure.

Marcus began threatening legal action, claiming co-ownership and decision-making rights. Without a written partnership agreement defining what a silent partner could and could not do, Frank had little protection. Despite being the sole operator, Marcus's financial contribution gave him leverage—and ambiguity worked in Marcus's favor.

To protect what he had built, Frank made a difficult decision: he chose to buy Marcus out completely.

But without a pre-agreed valuation or buyout clause, Marcus demanded far more than his original investment. The price had nothing to do with contribution—it was based on emotion, leverage, and opportunity. Exhausted and boxed in, Frank paid the amount just to regain full control of the company he had built alone from day one.

Marcus signed a release, officially severing ties.

Frank kept the business—but the cost was steep. Financially, emotionally, and mentally, the experience left its mark. Still, one thing was undeniable: **the business survived because Frank had built it without dependency on a silent partner who later wanted a voice he never earned**.

The Business Lessons

Frank's experience highlights a mistake many entrepreneurs make when accepting startup capital: **they underestimate the power of undefined roles**.

A silent partner is not a co-operator, co-manager, or co-decision-maker. A silent partner provides capital—not control. The moment that role is not clearly documented, silence becomes optional, and ownership becomes debatable.

Frank's lessons are clear:

1. Capital Does Not Equal Control

Marcus provided money, but Frank provided everything else—vision, labor, risk, relationships, and execution. Without Frank's daily involvement, there would have been no business to profit from. Funding alone does not justify operational authority unless it is explicitly granted.

2. Silent Partners Must Be Defined in Writing

A true silent partner has no role in daily operations, no authority over staff, and no unilateral decision-making power. When this is not documented, investors can later claim involvement they never earned.

3. The Builder Must Be Protected

Frank built the business from the ground up. He carried the stress, made the decisions, and assumed the risk. Entrepreneurs who build must protect their position through operating agreements that clearly establish who runs the business and who does not.

4. Growth Changes People

As the business became profitable, Marcus's expectations changed. This is common. Success often invites second thoughts, entitlement, and power grabs. Agreements must anticipate growth—not just the startup phase.

5. Buyouts Should Never Be Emotional

Because there was no buyout clause or valuation formula, Marcus was able to name his price. Frank paid more than he should have—not because it was fair, but because it was necessary to protect his company.

6. Independence Saved the Business

The reason Frank's company survived the split is simple: it was never dependent on the silent partner to function. Frank built systems, relationships, and operations that stood on their own. That independence gave him leverage when everything else was uncertain.

Conclusion

Frank didn't lose his business—but he paid a steep price to keep it.

His story is not a warning against accepting help; it is a warning against accepting help **without boundaries**. Silent partners are not dangerous—**undefined silent partners are**.

Entrepreneurs must remember this:

If you build the business, you must protect the business.

Structure is not distrust. Documentation is not disloyalty. Agreements do not weaken partnerships—they prevent destruction.

Frank walked away wiser, leaner, and fully in control of what he built. And this time, there was no confusion about who was silent—and who was in charge.

When Trust Overrides Structure

The Story: Lucky's Costly Lesson

Johnnie and Lucky were longtime friends who decided to go into business together. Johnnie was a licensed truck driver with years of experience in logistics. Lucky, on the other hand, had strong credit and financial resources, so he agreed to fund the business. He purchased a semi-truck for Johnnie to drive, financed several additional trucks, and together they launched their transportation company.

Johnnie was responsible for operations, managing routes, scheduling drivers, and handling finances. Lucky trusted Johnnie completely and allowed him access to the company bank account. But as payments from delivery contracts started rolling in, Johnnie quietly began transferring funds into his personal account. From there, he would pay the drivers himself without any formal payroll system.

Lucky had no idea. He focused on his other ventures and let Johnnie handle the trucking side.

That is, until tax season.

When Lucky filed taxes for his other businesses, the IRS flagged a discrepancy: a 1099 had been issued in his name for over $300,000 under the trucking company. Confused, Lucky requested full documentation from Johnnie. What he discovered was shocking: Johnnie had been using the business income for personal expenses, paying people informally, and keeping little to no record of transactions. Worse yet, lapses in truck insurance led to the termination of a major logistics contract, putting the entire company in jeopardy.

The confrontation between the two escalated. Lucky, trying to salvage the situation, hired a CPA who advised him to cut ties with Johnnie immediately and restructure the business. Johnnie promised to do better. He agreed to work with the CPA, and for three months, things improved: accounts were reconciled, insurance was maintained, and payroll was established properly.

But the change didn't last.

Johnnie slowly reverted to his old habits, bypassing systems and misusing business funds. Lucky, fed up and financially strained, was forced to shut the company down. Unfortunately, because there was no formal partnership agreement and all financial dealings were in Lucky's name, the IRS held him personally responsible for unpaid taxes and liabilities that spanned three years.

The business ended. The friendship was strained beyond repair. And Lucky was left with a heavy financial burden because he operated on trust instead of structure.

Business Lessons: Structure First, Friendship Second

1. **Never Launch a Business Without Legal Documentation**

   This case reinforces the need for a written and signed partnership agreement. It should clearly define ownership percentages, financial responsibilities, authority levels, and dispute resolution protocols.

2. **Keep Finances Separate and Transparent**

   No one partner should have sole access to the business bank account. Implement dual-authority controls, professional bookkeeping, and use accounting software to track transactions in real time. Personal accounts should never be used for business income or expenses.

3. **Formalize Payroll and Contractor Payments**

   All payments to staff or contractors must be properly documented, taxed, and reported. Failure to do so can result in IRS penalties and loss of trust with your workforce. Never run payroll off the books.

4. **Monitor and Maintain Compliance Obligations**

   Insurance lapses, unpaid taxes, and unrecorded transactions can destroy your business. Assign these responsibilities to a qualified third party such as a CPA or compliance manager and set calendar reminders for critical deadlines.

5. **File Business Formation Properly**

   Ensure the business is legally structured (LLC, partnership, or corporation) and registered with the proper authorities. If only one name is associated with the business on official documents, that individual assumes all liability, as Lucky did.

6. **Act Quickly on Red Flags**

   When signs of financial mismanagement appear, don't delay. Address them immediately. Waiting too long can cost you thousands in taxes, penalties, and legal fees.

Final Thought

In business, good intentions are not enough. Friendship does not replace financial accountability, and verbal agreements are no substitute for structured, legal foundations. Lucky learned too late that overlooking documentation and financial transparency can create consequences that extend far beyond business into personal credit, legal liability, and long-term financial stability.

The Beauty of Business... and the Cost of Blind Spots

The Story: Shelley's Salon Setback

Shelley and Patricia had worked side by side for years in a busy hair salon, often dreaming aloud about opening a place of their own. Both were talented, passionate, and eager to build something they could call their own. When Shelley found a commercial space that was perfect for a beauty studio, she immediately shared the news with Patricia. They both agreed to go in as 50/50 partners.

Patricia moved fast and secured the lease, and by the time Shelley joined, her name was simply added on as a co-owner of the business. Though the arrangement wasn't formally written out in detail, both women understood it: they would share financial responsibilities and contribute equally by servicing clients and managing the salon.

For the first several months, the salon flourished. Clients were steady, and the bills were paid. But about nine months in, Shelley noticed Patricia's absence. She had stopped showing up consistently and wasn't pulling her weight. Shelley was suddenly left to manage the day-to-day operations, cover expenses, and keep the energy of the salon alive.

After four months of handling it alone, Shelley finally sat down with Patricia to ask what was going on. Patricia confessed she was dealing with personal matters and no longer wanted to be involved. She told Shelley she could have the business, no payment needed, no strings attached.

Trusting that the handoff was clean, Shelley took over completely.

However, Patricia then contacted the landlord without Shelley's knowledge and requested that her name be removed from the lease, stating that Shelley was now solely responsible. The landlord made the change with no discussion or acknowledgment from Shelley.

A few years later, as the economy shifted and business declined, Shelley made the difficult decision to close the salon. But when she notified the landlord, she was told the lease was still in effect and was a 10-year commercial lease with no early-termination clause.

The landlord sued Shelley for breach of contract and pursued her personal assets, her home and other businesses. Shelley was shocked. She argued that she was not the original leaseholder and never signed a 10-year agreement. But legally, her name was the only one on the lease, thanks to Patricia's removal request and the landlord's unilateral update.

In the end, Shelley had no choice but to file for bankruptcy to protect herself and her remaining assets. The experience left her feeling deceived, legally trapped, and painfully aware of what she didn't know when she entered the partnership.

The Solutions: Protecting Yourself in Partnerships and Commercial Leases

1. **Never Rely on Verbal Agreements, Formalize Every Detail**

   A clear and legally binding partnership agreement should cover ownership percentages, roles, buyout terms, exit strategies, and what happens if one party walks away.

2. **Understand Lease Terms Before Signing**

Commercial leases are often long-term and difficult to exit. Always review leases with an attorney before signing and clarify who is liable if one party leaves.

3. **Maintain Written Consent for Any Ownership or Lease Changes**

   If a partner leaves or roles change, update all documents legally. Never allow someone to remove or change names on legal documents without your knowledge or written approval.

4. **Always Consult Legal Counsel Before Accepting Full Responsibility**

   When Patricia offered the business for free, Shelley should have involved an attorney to structure a formal transfer of ownership and responsibility.

5. **Establish an Operating Agreement or LLC Structure**

   An LLC with a proper operating agreement can help protect personal assets and define member roles.

6. **Know Your Exit Rights in Commercial Leases**

   Negotiate early termination clauses or subleasing options in your commercial lease.

7. **Document All Changes and Keep Personal Records**

   Every agreement, lease change, or ownership transfer should be documented. Without written proof, verbal promises have no standing in court.

Final Thought

Shelley's story is one that echoes across industries: trusting too much, assuming good intentions are enough, and not knowing the legal weight of documents. Passion will get you started, but paperwork protects you when things go south. Partnerships without structure are just risks wrapped in good intentions.

Partnership Readiness Checklist and Lease Review Guide

This tool is designed to help entrepreneurs avoid the common legal and operational mistakes covered in Chapter 10.

Partnership Readiness Checklist

Before entering any business partnership, ensure the following documents and agreements are in place:

- **Legal and Ownership**
    - Partnership Agreement signed by all partners
    - Clear ownership percentages and profit/loss distribution
    - Defined capital contributions
    - Terms for partner withdrawal, death, or default
    - Non-compete and confidentiality clauses if applicable
- **Operations and Management**
    - Defined roles and responsibilities
    - Voting rights or decision-making authority
    - Dispute resolution process
    - Guidelines for hiring, firing, and HR matters
    - Procedure for accessing bank accounts and financial systems
- **Financial Protections**

    - Separate business bank account
    - Budget and operating expense plan
    - Agreement on bookkeeping and CPA oversight
    - Tax responsibilities outlined
    - Buy-sell agreement with valuation formula
- **Lease Review Guide for Co-Founders**
- Before signing or transferring responsibility for a commercial lease:
- **Lease Review Essentials**
    - Lease term
    - Monthly rent and escalation clauses
    - Personal guarantor clause
    - Termination clause
    - Renewal options
- **Legal Protections**
    - All leaseholders must sign any amendment
    - Landlord acknowledges any transfer
    - Documented proof of communications
    - Business registered to a legal entity
- **Partner Exit and Lease Implications**
    - What happens if a partner leaves
    - Written process for lease transfer
    - Subletting or selling the business options
- **Final Reminders**
    - If it's not in writing, it doesn't exist legally
    - Always consult a business attorney
    - Partnerships fail more from poor documentation than bad business

Conclusion: Partnerships Require More Than Good Intentions

Each of the three stories in this chapter shares a painful truth that many entrepreneurs learn too late: trust without structure is a liability, not an asset.

Frank believed that loyalty and verbal agreements with a close friend would be enough to protect him in business, only to realize that success can shift people's intentions. Lucky trusted Johnnie to operate with integrity, but a lack of oversight and documentation left him buried in tax debt. Shelley entered a partnership based on a shared dream but didn't protect herself legally, resulting in financial ruin.

The lesson is simple: business partnerships must be approached with rigor and formality. Passion and trust are wonderful starting points, but they are no substitute for written agreements, defined roles, and legal protections.

Whether it's the excitement of launching a new venture or the comfort of working with someone you know, don't let emotions cloud your judgment. Protect your business, your assets, and your peace of mind by doing the legal work upfront. It's not about expecting failure, it's about preparing for real life.

Chapter 11
When Trust Costs You

Niece had always dreamed of owning her own boutique. What started as an online business selling handpicked, hard-to-find pieces quickly evolved into a small storefront filled with unique clothing and accessories. She poured her heart and soul into setting up the shop, personally hanging merchandise, managing customer service, and handling all the behind-the-scenes logistics.

At first, she ran everything on her own, but as business picked up, she brought on help. A cashier was hired to manage the front of the store, and an evening clerk was brought in to receive deliveries, tag merchandise, and stock the store. Niece was proud of the boutique's progress. While profits weren't overwhelming, the store was self-sufficient, covering its expenses and leaving a modest profit behind.

At first, she performed inventory counts every month. But as operations became smoother and she felt more comfortable, she moved to quarterly inventory reviews. During a routine meeting with her accountant, a red flag arose. When asked how she was determining her pricing, Niece referenced her markup strategy and shared her tracking spreadsheet. However, her accountant noticed discrepancies in the profit margins.

Together, they decided to input the inventory data into accounting software to get a clearer picture. To their surprise, several items were missing, products that were listed on her spreadsheet but no longer appeared in the store. Concerned, Niece reviewed camera footage but saw no evidence of customers stealing merchandise.

To get to the bottom of the issue, she installed additional surveillance cameras near the cash register, in the back room, and in the delivery area. After a month of closely monitoring the footage, the truth came out.

The evening clerk had been collaborating with the delivery driver. The clerk would sign off on receiving four boxes, but only three would be unloaded. Meanwhile, the cashier was pocketing cash from the register. The niece noticed instances in which the cashier would pretend to make change from her purse but would take more than she returned.

Heartbroken by the betrayal, Niece terminated both employees and temporarily returned to managing the store by herself. Once she hired new staff, she implemented stronger internal controls, including inventory checklists, camera reviews, cash register audits, and documented delivery procedures.

Over time, her new systems proved successful. Niece learned that as her business grew, so did the need for constant evaluation and improvements in the process. It wasn't just about selling unique products, it was about protecting her dream from internal threats.

Solutions and Lessons Learned:

1. **Establish Strong Internal Controls Early:**
2. Even in small businesses, clearly documented procedures and regular checks can prevent theft or loss.
3. Require dual verification for deliveries, one person receives, another counts and checks against invoices.
4. **Implement Regular Audits and Inventory Counts:**
5. Stick to a monthly inventory schedule to catch discrepancies early.
6. Random spot checks in between scheduled audits can serve as a deterrent.
7. **Use Technology as a Preventative Tool:**

8. Invest in camera surveillance not just for customer areas but also for back-of-house operations like deliveries and inventory rooms.
9. Consider integrating POS systems that match cash flow with inventory movement for real-time tracking.
10. **Monitor Cash Handling Closely:**
11. Limit access to the cash register and require register logins for every transaction.
12. Reconcile cash drawers daily and compare sales reports to deposits.
13. **Create a Culture of Accountability:**
14. Train employees in ethical behavior and the consequences of theft.
15. Encourage transparency and have all employees sign policies that outline expectations around inventory and cash handling.
16. **Hire Slowly, Fire Quickly, but Document Thoroughly:**
17. Conduct background checks and provide proper training.
18. If issues arise, document everything and act quickly to protect the business.
19. **Review and Evolve Your Processes:**
20. What works when you're small might not work as you grow. Niece's success came from continuously updating her systems to match the needs of a growing business.

Niece's experience is a powerful reminder that growth brings both opportunity and responsibility. While her boutique began as a passion project built on trust and hard work, it quickly revealed the importance of oversight, accountability, and structured systems. Trust alone is not a substitute for controls, and every business, no matter how small, needs safeguards in place to protect its operations.

Through the challenges of employee theft and inventory loss, Niece didn't give up. Instead, she responded like a true entrepreneur, acting, adjusting her approach, and reinforcing her business with better processes. Her story teaches us that setbacks can serve as valuable turning points when we choose to learn from them. With clear systems, constant vigilance, and the courage to adapt, business owners can not only recover from internal missteps but also come back stronger and more prepared for future success.

Building Loyalty Through Leadership

Manny owned a small but bustling 24-hour smoke shop that sold the latest smoke pens, gadgets, and flavored products. Business was steady, and the demand for his merchandise remained high. However, behind the scenes, Manny struggled with a recurring issue, employee theft and high turnover.

He had six employees on rotating shifts, but many of them treated the store inventory as their own. Manny found himself checking the cash register multiple times a day and reviewing security camera footage frequently. Even with cabinets and clearly labeled inventory, theft persisted. The most frustrating part was watching employees casually use new smoke pens without paying for them.

One employee seemed to have a new pen every other day. When confronted, the employee insisted he had purchased them elsewhere. Manny didn't fully believe him, but he also felt trapped. People needed to cover the overnight shifts, and firing someone meant dealing with another hiring process he didn't have time for.

Feeling overwhelmed, Manny hired a consultant with retail management experience to help restructure the store operations and reduce theft. Together, they created a more efficient workflow and introduced clear accountability systems.

Manny also implemented an employee incentive program. Staff members who met sales quotas would receive cash rewards or free merchandise. He introduced quarterly bonuses tied directly to store performance, which motivated employees to run transactions properly through the register. As sales increased and theft decreased, morale improved.

To build trust and create a better work environment, Manny started hosting company dinners and held an annual holiday celebration. He made a conscious effort to check in with each employee personally, asking about their goals, challenges, and home life. This human connection started to shift the store culture.

Eventually, Manny confronted the employee he had long suspected of stealing. To his surprise, the employee admitted to taking the pens. He explained that he felt underappreciated and invisible, like Manny only kept him around because no one else would work overnight. However, he also acknowledged that things had changed. He appreciated the incentives, the team dinners, and the way Manny had started showing genuine interest in his staff. He admitted he had been wrong and expressed gratitude for the way things were turning around.

Solutions and Lessons Learned:

1. **Recognize That People Want to Feel Valued:**
2. Employee theft is often not just about money or products, it's about feeling unseen or unappreciated.
3. Building relationships with your staff fosters trust and loyalty.
4. **Implement Accountability Systems:**
5. Secure your inventory with locked cabinets and frequent checks.
6. Rotate and audit registers often, and monitor footage, but pair surveillance with staff engagement, not suspicion alone.
7. **Incentivize Positive Behavior:**
8. Performance-based bonuses and rewards for meeting sales goals give employees a reason to care about the bottom line.
9. When employees know their efforts are tied to real benefits, they're less likely to steal and more likely to drive sales.
10. **Invest in Leadership and Training:**

11. Bringing in a retail management consultant gave Manny fresh perspective and tools he didn't have before.
12. Training promotes consistency and professionalism, especially in high-turnover industries.
13. **Create a Culture, Not Just a Schedule:**
14. Company events, team dinners, and honest conversations go a long way.
15. Employees are less likely to steal from a business they feel emotionally invested in.

Conclusion:

Manny's journey highlights a crucial truth in business management: people are at the heart of your operations. While systems and technology are important, it's how you lead and engage with your team that determines the strength of your business culture. By taking the time to restructure his store, offer incentives, and build personal connections, Manny transformed his workplace from a revolving door of distrust to a motivated, loyal team.

He learned that leadership isn't just about assigning shifts, it's about setting the tone, earning respect, and giving people a reason to believe in the business they're part of. Manny's shift in mindset didn't just reduce theft, it strengthened his entire operation for long-term success.

Betrayal Behind the Counter

Andy inherited his family's beloved candy shop, a small-town staple known for its charm and sweet treats. Out of tradition and community pride, he continued his parents' practice of hiring local students, high schoolers and a few college kids, to give them work experience and some extra cash. Among his hires was a young man from the neighborhood, brought on as a favor to his mother, who had asked Andy to help her son stay out of trouble.

At first, everything ran smoothly. The young man was polite, punctual, and well-liked. In fact, Andy noticed more foot traffic than usual during the boy's shifts. Groups of people, mostly young adults, would come in frequently, but oddly, only when the young man was working. Andy appreciated the steady business, so he didn't question it too much. Sales were steady, and no obvious signs of theft appeared.

However, things started to feel strange. One day, several customers came in asking for the young man by name. When Andy informed them that he wasn't working that day and offered to help, they declined and left. That moment planted a seed of suspicion.

The next day, Andy quietly observed. Customers streamed in again, talking only to the young man, who would grab a bottle of water or a small candy bar, ring it up, chat briefly, and hand over a bag. Curious, Andy reviewed surveillance footage and noticed the same subtle pattern repeating, every transaction involving the young man was accompanied by a suspicious exchange, always ending in a bagged item.

During a break, Andy searched under the counter for anything hidden but found nothing and reluctantly let it go.

A few days later, two officers came into the store and asked to speak with the young man outside. When he returned, Andy asked what it was about, and the young man casually brushed it off as "just questions about something that happened in the neighborhood."

Later that day, after watching another interaction unfold, Andy stopped one of the customers before she left the store. Nervously, she hesitated when he asked to inspect her bag. Inside, amid a few candy items, was a small plastic bag filled with illegal substances.

Devastated, Andy confronted the young man in the back room. The confrontation was heated. Andy demanded he leave and never return. Two days later, the police returned, informing Andy that the shop had been under investigation due to reported drug activity. His heart sank. He felt like everything his parents had built was on the verge of collapse.

Andy called the young man and his mother in to speak with the authorities. To his credit, the young man admitted that Andy was not involved and that the drug activity was conducted without his knowledge. That statement cleared Andy from criminal liability, but the experience left a lasting scar.

Afterward, Andy found it hard to trust any employee. He became a micromanager, watching over every move, double-checking transactions, and reviewing camera footage daily. Though he avoided legal trouble, the emotional and reputational toll was heavy.

Solutions and Lessons Learned:

1. **Conduct Thorough Background Checks:**

    o Even when hiring community members or doing favors, ensure you understand who you're bringing into your business.

    o Don't skip proper screening, no matter how harmless the hire may seem.

2. **Establish Clear Policies and Monitoring:**

    o Create written employee conduct policies, including zero tolerance for illegal activity.

    o Set clear boundaries for what is allowed behind the counter and monitor daily operations.

3. **Use Technology Intelligently:**

   o Surveillance cameras are only useful when reviewed and paired with secure inventory and cash register processes.

   o POS systems should track all items sold and associate them with employee IDs.

4. **Be Proactive with Law Enforcement:**

   o If suspicious activity arises, proactively contact authorities rather than waiting for them to show up.

   o Cooperation can protect your business and show that you are not complicit.

5. **Develop a Trust-Building Onboarding Process:**

   o Create a structured onboarding and training system to instill expectations and trust from the beginning.

   o Empower employees with responsibility, but don't shy away from enforcing accountability.

Conclusion:

Andy's story reveals a harsh reality: even a business built on legacy and good intentions is not immune to being exploited. While Andy's compassion and desire to help a young man led him to give someone a chance, it also opened the door for illegal activity that nearly destroyed his shop.

His experience underscores the importance of balancing trust with accountability. As a business owner, it's essential to establish clear expectations, monitor employee behavior consistently, and maintain the integrity of your business, no matter who is working for you. Andy's painful lesson taught him to never ignore red flags, to trust his instincts, and to protect what his family worked so hard to build.

Though the betrayal hurt, Andy emerged wiser, stronger, and more aware. His story is a reminder to entrepreneurs everywhere that leadership means not just being kind, but being vigilant too.

Conclusion

The stories of Niece, Manny, and Andy serve as powerful and sobering reminders that trust, while essential in business, must be balanced with structure, accountability, and strong leadership. Each of them faced a different form of internal betrayal, from employee theft and manipulation to criminal activity, all of which could have severely damaged or even destroyed their businesses.

Niece learned that as her boutique grew, so did the need for improved systems and tighter inventory controls. Manny discovered that investing in people and cultivating a culture of recognition and accountability could shift employee behavior and improve store morale. Andy was confronted with the painful reality that even good intentions and community loyalty aren't enough to safeguard a business from those who choose to exploit opportunity.

What ties these stories together is the critical lesson that every entrepreneur must put protections in place, whether through technology, policy, or employee development, to preserve the integrity of their brand and operations. Leadership is not just about managing a store or assigning tasks; it's about setting the tone, enforcing boundaries, and making tough decisions when needed.

These business owners all rose from their challenges stronger and more resilient. Their stories reflect the emotional, legal, and financial consequences of internal breakdowns, but more importantly, they reveal the power of corrective action and learning from experience.

In business, mistakes are inevitable, but how you respond to them is what defines your success.

Chapter 12
The Illusion of Wealth

The Story

Tina had built a reputation for running one of the most stylish salons in her city. Her chairs were always full, her books stayed booked weeks in advance, and her clients were fiercely loyal. From the outside looking in, Tina appeared to be the definition of success. She drove luxury cars, wore designer labels, and regularly posted photos on social media showcasing lavish vacations and high-end purchases. To the public, Tina was thriving.

But behind the scenes, her financial reality told a very different story.

For years, Tina cut corners where no one could see. Instead of placing her stylists on payroll, she paid them as independent contractors—even though they worked set schedules, used her equipment, followed her rules, and depended on her salon for income. She justified it as "industry standard" and told herself she was avoiding unnecessary expenses. What she was really avoiding were payroll taxes, unemployment insurance, and employer responsibilities.

When it came time to file taxes, Tina took another shortcut.

She consistently overstated business expenses and aggressively wrote off personal costs as business deductions. Hair, clothing, travel, meals, vehicles—anything that could be justified, even loosely, was expensed. By overstating deductions and underreporting income, Tina often received refunds instead of paying what she truly owed. In the short term, it felt like a win. More cash stayed in her pocket. More money funded the lifestyle she wanted others to see.

But the numbers on her tax returns didn't match the success she portrayed.

Year after year, Tina filed late or filed just enough income to avoid raising alarms. She never thought about Social Security contributions, retirement credits, or the long-term consequences of reporting low income. As far as she was concerned, that was a problem for "later."

Later came sooner than she expected.

When business slowed and Tina had to let a stylist go, that former worker filed for unemployment. That single claim triggered a state labor board investigation. The audit revealed what Tina had ignored for years: employee misclassification.

The state labor department audited her books, payroll records, and tax filings. The penalties were severe—back payroll taxes, unemployment contributions, interest, fines, and reclassification costs. What Tina thought she had saved over the years disappeared almost overnight. Legal fees and accounting costs piled on. The financial pressure was relentless.

The stress took a toll.

Tina became physically ill. Anxiety turned into chronic health issues. Running the salon became exhausting, then impossible. The business she once controlled now controlled her—and her body could no longer keep up.

In her late sixties, Tina finally stepped away and applied for Social Security benefits, believing her decades of work would carry her through retirement. Instead, she learned she qualified for only $550 per month—a direct result of years of underreporting income and failing to pay into the system properly.

Shocked, she applied for disability and was approved for $900 per month. It wasn't enough to sustain the lifestyle she once displayed online. Tina sold her luxury car, moved into low-income housing, and relied on public assistance to survive. The designer bags, vacations, and image of wealth were gone.

What remained were the consequences of financial shortcuts she once believed were smart business decisions.

The Business Lessons

Tina's story illustrates how short-term financial manipulation creates long-term devastation.

1. Misclassifying Employees Is Not a Strategy

Paying employees as contractors to avoid payroll taxes exposes your business to audits, penalties, and back payments. One unemployment claim is all it takes to trigger an investigation.

2. Overstating Expenses Creates a False Sense of Wealth

Using excessive or improper deductions may result in refunds today, but it lowers your reported income—directly impacting loans, retirement benefits, and Social Security eligibility.

3. Refunds Can Be a Red Flag

Consistent tax refunds for a profitable cash-based business often signal overuse of deductions or underreported income. Refunds feel good now but can destroy your future.

4. Social Security Is Earned, Not Guaranteed

Your benefits are based on what you report and contribute. Filing low income today means low benefits tomorrow—no exceptions.

5. Audits Don't Just Cost Money—they Cost Health

The financial strain of audits, penalties, and legal battles can lead to burnout, stress-related illness, and loss of control over both business and life.

6. Lifestyle Is Not the Same as Stability

A business that funds appearances through deception is not profitable—it is fragile.

Conclusion: The True Cost of the Illusion

Tina didn't fail because she lacked talent or ambition. She failed because she chose appearance over structure and refunds over responsibility.

Her story is a reminder that wealth built on shortcuts is temporary, but the consequences are permanent. True success isn't what you post online—it's what your financials say when the spotlight is gone.

Entrepreneurs must choose wisely:

Legacy over lifestyle. Compliance over convenience. Planning over illusion.

Because one day, the business will slow down. Your body will need rest. And what you reported—or failed to report—will determine how well your future is protected.

Build it right the first time. Your future self is depending on it.

The Cost of Cutting Corners

Dean was well-known in his community as the guy who could fix any car. His auto shop stayed busy, and from the outside, he appeared to be doing exceptionally well. He drove high-end vehicles, dressed the part of a successful entrepreneur, and spoke confidently about "his" home in a prestigious neighborhood. What many didn't know, however, was that the cars were financed to the limit and the house was a rental with a hefty monthly payment.

Dean, like many small business owners operating in cash-heavy industries, chose to bypass the traditional rules. He paid his staff as independent contractors to avoid responsibility for payroll taxes and workers' compensation. He didn't keep accurate books and often pocketed cash without recording it. Tax filing was never a priority; I only filed when necessary and usually late.

The turning point came when his wife, tired of renting, decided it was time for them to buy a home. She began the mortgage application process, believing they were more than financially ready. But when the loan officer reviewed their documentation, the application hit a brick wall. Dean didn't have the financial records to prove enough income for loan approval.

Desperate to save the deal, Dean went to an accountant and asked for help. The accountant began reconstructing his books, requesting bank statements, invoices, and most important, proof of income. Dean admitted he had collected a large portion of his income in cash and had never deposited it into a bank account. However, he did keep daily records through his point-of-sale system, which revealed the true volume of business he'd been doing.

The accountant worked diligently to rebuild the financials, but the process was long and expensive. In the end, the accounting bill was thousands of dollars, and that wasn't even the worst part. The IRS was now involved, and Dean was hit with a $65,000 tax liability for the years of underreported income. At that point, buying a home was no longer an option. Dean had to shift his focus from acquiring new assets to cleaning up the financial mess he had created.

Solution: Building Financial Credibility, the Right Way

Dean's story highlights how under-the-table operations can sabotage long-term goals. Many entrepreneurs in cash-driven businesses fall into the same trap, avoiding taxes today only to pay dearly in the future. Here's how to fix and avoid this costly mistake:

1. **Operate Above Board**

   Pay employees correctly and classify them accurately. Misclassifying workers not only affects your taxes but could also result in penalties and lawsuits.

2. **Report All Income, Even Cash**

   Income not deposited or tracked is considered invisible when applying for credit, loans, or investment opportunities. Use a POS system that records all sales and deposit cash consistently to establish financial credibility.

3. **Keep Accurate Financial Records**

   Hire a bookkeeper or accountant who can help you maintain clean books year-round, not just when you're in crisis. Regular financial reporting allows you to make informed business decisions and prepares you for opportunities.

4. **File Taxes on Time**

   Late filings and unpaid taxes accumulate interest and penalties. Consistently filing on time helps you stay in good standing with lenders, government agencies, and partners.

5. **Think Long-Term**

   If your personal goals include owning a home, expanding your business, or obtaining financing, your financial documentation must reflect stability and legitimacy.

Conclusion: Don't Let Your Dreams Die in the Details

Dean's lifestyle looked successful, but it was built on a shaky foundation. His failure to run his business with integrity delayed his family's dream of homeownership and saddled him with overwhelming tax debt.

Success isn't just about what people see, it's about what your financials say. If your books tell a different story from your lifestyle, eventually the truth will surface.

The takeaway is clear: real wealth is built through structure, documentation, and compliance. Don't let shortcuts today cost you your future tomorrow. Invest in the systems and professionals that will help your business thrive, not just on paper, but in reality.

When "Doing Everything Right" Isn't Enough

Curt ran a thriving trucking business. With years of industry knowledge under his belt, he built a strong reputation and consistently brought in substantial income. He operated with integrity, treated his drivers well, and followed industry standards by classifying them as independent contractors, since they had full control over their schedules.

Curt was the kind of entrepreneur who believed in doing things the right way. He filed his taxes every year and paid what his accountant told him he owed without question. On paper, everything seemed to be handled responsibly.

After several successful years in business, Curt and his wife decided it was time to purchase their first home. They were excited and confident that with Curt's strong income, the process would be smooth. But during the loan application process, their real estate agent came back with news that stunned them both.

Although Curt had earned $380,000 the previous year, his accountant had claimed $370,000 in expenses. On paper, Curt had only made $10,000, which made him ineligible for the loan.

Curt was floored. "How could this be?" he asked.

The real estate agent sat him down and explained the problem. She emphasized that while Curt's business was profitable, the over-deduction in expenses made it appear otherwise to lenders. The expenses weren't necessarily false, but they hadn't been reviewed with Curt strategically, nor had they been optimized with future goals like homeownership in mind.

The real estate agent referred Curt to a more experienced accountant who specialized in working with business owners. The new accountant reviewed his books, identified areas of excess deductions, and amended the tax returns. The amendments raised Curt's taxable income to a realistic level, allowing him to qualify for the mortgage. However, they also triggered a tax bill of $25,000.

Curt paid the IRS and took the situation as a valuable learning opportunity. He retained the new accountant for monthly bookkeeping and tax planning. They restructured his business as an S Corporation, placed him on payroll, and began generating financial statements that reflected both accuracy and strength.

By the following year, Curt's tax liability dropped to under $4,000, and his reported income increased, thanks to the combination of W-2 wages and a shareholder K-1. Not only did this strategy improve his tax position, but it also laid the foundation for long-term financial credibility, allowing him to plan with confidence for future investments and retirement.

Solution: Don't Just File, Strategize

Curt's story shows that even when business owners operate ethically, they can still face setbacks if they lack proactive financial planning. Here's how to avoid this common pitfall:

1. **Review Financials with Purpose**

   Tax preparation should be a conversation, not a transaction. Entrepreneurs must work with professionals who understand their short- and long-term goals and tailor deductions and filings accordingly.

2. **Choose an Accountant Who Understands Your Industry**

   Not all accountants are created equal. You need someone who understands business structure, growth planning, and the balance between tax minimization and financial credibility.

3. **Amend When Necessary, But Learn from It**

   Amending returns is sometimes necessary to correct issues or reposition your finances, but it should be used as a learning tool, not a recurring strategy.

4. **Structure Matters**

Curt's switch to an S Corporation improved his tax positioning and allowed him to reduce his tax liability while still reporting meaningful income legally.

5. **Bookkeeping Isn't Optional**

   Accurate monthly bookkeeping helps you understand where your money is going and ensures your business always stays loan- and investment-ready.

Conclusion: Financial Intelligence Is Financial Power

Curt did everything he thought was right; he paid his taxes, ran an honest business, and stayed within the law. But without active tax planning and financial strategy, he still found himself unprepared when it mattered most.

The lesson here is simple: it's not enough to just "stay out of trouble." To build real wealth and security, business owners must engage in forward-thinking financial planning. You need a team that not only reports the numbers but also helps you use those numbers to move forward.

Curt's story ends with success, not because he avoided mistakes, but because he corrected them and built a stronger foundation moving forward.

When Growth Reveals the Gaps

Maria had built an impressive med spa brand with multiple locations across several states. Her services were in high demand, and her business was expanding rapidly. She had a combination of W-2 employees and independent contractors, and she filed her taxes each year without fail. From the outside, Maria looked like she had it all under control.

As her business gained more traction, Maria began the process of opening a new location in another state. During the initial setup, the new state requested her tax returns and corporate documents for verification. Confident in her track record, Maria submitted the documents without hesitation.

Once she successfully opened her new location, Maria decided it was time to bring on a more experienced accountant to handle the complexity of her growing enterprise. The new accountant immediately requested all her prior tax filings and business formation documents.

Maria sent over everything. A few weeks later, she was asked to come in for a meeting. What she learned in that meeting left her stunned.

Her business had been initially set up as a C Corporation, which required it to file its own corporate tax returns using IRS Form 1120. However, for years, her previous accountant had incorrectly reported all the business income on her personal tax return as if it were a sole proprietorship or disregarded entity. As a result, no corporate returns had ever been filed.

This error led to multiple years of missed filings, late penalties, and interest for the corporation. The new accountant had to act fast. First, they prepared and filed corporate tax returns for each year that had been missed. Then, they amended her personal tax returns to remove the business income and report only her legitimate personal earnings.

The adjustments produced surprising results. Maria was entitled to a refund of over $50,000 on the personal side due to overreported income. However, she owed about $40,000 on the corporate side for back taxes and penalties. Though the amounts nearly offset each other, the process came with a hefty price tag; the accountant charged a significant fee to unravel and correct years of improper filings.

Solution: Know Your Entity, Know Your Obligations

Maria's story is a powerful reminder that as your business grows, so does the complexity of compliance. Even when you think everything is being handled correctly, one fundamental mistake can cause years of damage. Here are the key solutions:

1. **Understand Your Business Entity**

   Whether you are a C Corporation, S Corporation, LLC, or sole proprietor, each structure has unique tax responsibilities. Always verify that your accountant is filing according to the correct entity classification.

2. **Review Your Filings Annually**

   Don't assume everything is right just because taxes are being filed. Ask to review the type of return being filed and ensure it aligns with your business registration with the IRS and state agencies.

3. **Separate Business and Personal Finances**

   Business income for a corporation should not appear on personal tax returns unless properly distributed (for example, through W-2 wages or dividends). Comingling these can create compliance issues and inflated tax liabilities.

4. **Hire Experienced Professionals**

   As your business scales, so should your advisory team. Invest in accountants and tax professionals with multi-state and corporate experience. The right expertise is worth the investment and may save you thousands.

5. **Stay Proactive**

   Make a habit of reviewing your entity status, tax deadlines, and filing procedures every year, especially before expanding or making major financial moves.

Conclusion: What You Don't Know Can Hurt You

Maria was a disciplined businesswoman who filed her taxes each year, trusted her advisors, and believed she was compliant. Yet one major oversight in the structure of her business cost her time, money, and peace of mind.

The lesson? Trust, but verify. As entrepreneurs, we must remain actively engaged in the financial and structural side of our businesses. Growth brings more responsibility, and it's not just about revenue, it's about reporting it the right way.

Maria's story ends on a positive note because she acted quickly, corrected the issue, and built a stronger foundation moving forward. But her experience highlights the hidden risks of unchecked assumptions.

The Hidden Cost of Financial Neglect

The four stories in this chapter offer a sobering but necessary look at what happens when business owners, whether through negligence, misinformation, or simple oversight, fail to fully understand or manage their financial responsibilities. Tina, Dean, Curt, and Maria each represent a different scenario, yet they all shared one thing in common: their financial challenges were preventable.

- Tina manipulated her finances for short-term gains, only to find herself with little to show for it in retirement.
- Dean ignored bookkeeping and underreported income, which derailed his family's chance at homeownership and led to significant IRS debt.
- Curt, despite running a compliant business, trusted without verifying and learned that even "doing the right thing" needs strategic planning.
- Maria trusted her previous accountant to file appropriately, only to discover years of entity misfiling that could have compromised her expanding empire.

These aren't just stories about numbers; they are about consequences. Whether it's losing access to capital, missing out on homeownership, paying unnecessary penalties, or delaying retirement security, the cost of financial mismanagement often far outweighs the effort it takes to do things correctly from the beginning.

The key takeaways are clear:

- Understand your business structure and tax obligations.
- Invest in knowledgeable, proactive financial professionals.
- File timely and accurate returns with a strategy in mind.
- Treat your books as a living tool, not just a year-end task.

Success is not just about making money, it's about keeping it, growing it, and using it to build a secure future. As these stories illustrate, it's not enough to be profitable. You must also be compliant, strategic, and informed.

Don't wait for a crisis to find out what's wrong. Be the kind of business owner who builds with intention, corrects mistakes quickly, and lays a financial foundation that lasts a lifetime.

Because in business, and in life, what you don't know can hurt you. But what you choose to learn and fix can save you.

Chapter 13
The Hidden Bias in Business

Story: Tina's Quiet Shift

Tina ran a small but growing accounting firm that specialized in helping small businesses increase revenue and stay compliant. Her reputation for quality service was strong, and she took pride in delivering real value to entrepreneurs from all walks of life. Being in a large, multicultural city, Tina believed her client base would reflect the same diversity she saw in her community.

However, over time, Tina noticed a troubling pattern. During her firm's annual outreach and renewal season, there were subtle signs of hesitation from certain prospective clients once they learned she was the owner and an African American. Some would politely decline further contact, others would simply ghost the conversation after initial interest. Tina was deeply disappointed but not surprised. She had dealt with unconscious bias before, but this hit harder because it directly affected her business growth.

Rather than allowing this bias to become a barrier, Tina made a strategic but emotionally conflicted decision. She hired a Caucasian accountant to serve as the face of the firm during initial client outreach, particularly when she sensed bias might be at play. The plan worked. The new employee would meet with prospective clients, build rapport, and close deals. Once clients experienced the firm's exceptional service, they rarely cared who the owner was, especially after learning Tina was behind the firm's excellent results.

Still, Tina wrestled with the moral implications of her decision. Was she compromising her values or simply adapting to a market that wasn't always fair? Her solution may have involved a calculated presentation, but her intention was never to deceive, only to give her firm the chance it deserved.

Solution: Addressing Bias with Strategic Empowerment

Tina's experience sheds light on the reality that many minority business owners face: implicit bias that creates invisible hurdles in professional settings. Her solution, while unconventional, was a form of strategic empowerment. She didn't allow discrimination to dictate her firm's growth. Instead, she adapted in a way that prioritized business success while maintaining high-quality service.

However, the long-term solution can't be to hide one's identity. Tina began investing in educational efforts and community outreach to show her face proudly as the firm's owner. She published content on business platforms, participated in local business panels, and even started sharing success stories through social media. Over time, her visibility and transparency helped change perceptions. Clients began to approach the firm not because of who they thought was in charge, but because of the reputation Tina had built.

She also created opportunities within her firm to support other professionals of color, offering mentorship and resources to help them navigate similar challenges. Her initial decision may have been born of necessity, but her long-term plan was centered on transformation and leadership.

Conclusion: Turning Perception into Purpose

Tina's story is one of resilience and resourcefulness. While it is disheartening to think that race still influences business decisions, her journey reflects a broader truth: bias still exists, but it can be dismantled, not just endured.

Her choice to adapt was neither deceitful nor disempowering. It was tactical. But more importantly, she didn't stop there. Tina used her experience to drive change, challenge bias, and open doors for others. In doing so, she not only grew her firm but helped reshape how clients saw business ownership and talent.

Sometimes the smartest move isn't just to win the game, but to change the rules.

Lee's Fight Against Fear and Prejudice

Story: Prejudice Served Cold

Lee owned a beloved Chinese restaurant that had long been a staple in the local community. It was a family-run establishment where his wife, children, siblings, and even in-laws worked together to serve authentic dishes and create a warm, welcoming atmosphere. Business had been steady for years, and Lee took pride in both the quality of his food and the unity of his family.

But everything changed when the COVID-19 pandemic hit.

Like many small businesses, Lee had no choice but to close the restaurant temporarily. While the government's PPP loans and SBA assistance helped them stay afloat during the shutdown, the real challenge came after restrictions were lifted. When Lee reopened the doors, the world he once knew had shifted, and not in his favor.

There was an undercurrent of hostility in the air. Due to widespread misinformation and misplaced blame about the virus, many people began to associate Asian-owned businesses with the pandemic unfairly. Lee and his family faced cruel remarks, cold shoulders, and a steep decline in customers. It wasn't just slow business, it was personal. People who had once been regulars now avoided the restaurant entirely, and some even left hateful comments online.

Lee was devastated. He questioned whether the years of service, sacrifice, and community involvement meant anything anymore. He contemplated closing permanently, unsure if the restaurant or his family could withstand the weight of ignorance and racism.

But his wife, wise and steady, urged him not to give up. "Let's be patient," she said. "Let's adapt. Let's outlast this hate."

They began offering deep discounts and weekly specials to attract new customers. They partnered with food delivery platforms, redesigned their packaging, and promoted their dishes online. Lee focused on the quality of the food and the loyalty of the few customers who still supported them. Slowly but surely, the tide began to turn.

The community's trust returned, not all at once, but steadily enough to keep the doors open. Business picked up, and Lee learned a difficult but powerful lesson.

Solution: Adapting Resilience and Strategy

Lee's restaurant didn't survive because of luck. It survived because of patience, strategy, and heart. Faced with unjust blame and xenophobia, Lee didn't retaliate or retreat. He recalibrated.

The use of food delivery services allowed him to reach customers in the comfort and safety of their homes, minimizing face-to-face interactions during a tense time. Strategic pricing and promotions encouraged people to give the food a chance again. But most importantly, Lee focused on maintaining his standards and never compromising the integrity of his service.

He also became more proactive financially, saving more aggressively and setting up contingency funds in the event of future downturns. By not allowing the hate to harden his spirit, Lee turned a moment of discrimination into a foundation of resilience.

Conclusion: Strength in Culture and Courage

Lee's story is a reminder that racism doesn't just hurt feelings. It impacts families, livelihoods, and legacies. But it's also a story of hope. In the face of widespread fear and blame, Lee held onto his dignity, adapted his business, and protected his family's dream.

His journey wasn't easy, and it wasn't fair, but it was victorious.

Today, his restaurant continues to grow. The dining room is once again full of laughter and conversation. Lee has not only rebuilt his business, he has fortified it. He now educates other business owners on emergency preparedness, advocates for diversity in entrepreneurship, and speaks openly about the impact of cultural prejudice on small businesses.

Lee's strength didn't come from avoiding the problem. It came from facing it with wisdom, love, and perseverance.

Sometimes, the best way to overcome hate is to outlast it with excellence.

Tammy's Thread of Purpose

Story: The Fashion of Faith

Tammy had always loved fashion. From a young age, she saw clothing not just as fabric but as a form of expression to help others feel confident, beautiful, and seen. In high school, her passion blossomed into purpose. She would design dresses for her classmates, often at little to no cost, simply because she loved seeing their joy when they wore her creations. Prom season was her busiest time, and her designs were the talk of the campus.

With the loving support of her mother, Tammy opened a small boutique right after high school. Her dream was unfolding in front of her, but not without challenges.

Tammy was a young woman with special needs, and while her talent was undeniable, her appearance and communication style often caused people to overlook her. Many assumed that her mother was the true owner of the boutique. When they learned that Tammy was the designer, some customers quietly walked away, doubting her ability solely because of her disability.

The rejection crushed Tammy. Her joy in creating started to dim. She became withdrawn and discouraged, questioning whether her dream was meant to survive.

One quiet afternoon, her mother sat beside her and asked, "Tammy, why do you make dresses?"

With her eyes downcast, Tammy softly replied, "Because I love making dresses and clothes."

Her mother smiled. "Then create because you love it, not for anyone else's approval. Let the rest work itself out."

Tammy took those words to heart. She began designing dresses simply for the joy of it again. She placed them proudly in the boutique window, no price tags, with no expectations. Her passion returned stitch by stitch.

People started noticing. They would stop and admire the dresses in the window. Soon, they were coming into the boutique asking about prices, and to Tammy's surprise, the dresses started selling regularly, without question and without doubt.

Then one day, a gentleman entered the boutique, admiring the detail in a particular gown. He asked to speak to the designer. Tammy's mother introduced him to Tammy. The man was impressed and immediately asked if she could create a bulk order of the design for an upcoming event.

A contract was drafted, and that order turned into a long-term relationship. Tammy eventually expanded her boutique into a small factory with employees. Today, she designs for clients across the country, and her work is featured in fashion showcases and community events.

Solution: Focusing on Passion, Not Prejudice

Tammy's journey is a powerful reminder that ability should never be judged by appearance. Rather than allow the ignorance of others to dictate her value, Tammy leaned into her purpose, supported by a mother who believed in her potential.

The turning point came when she stopped chasing approval and started creating purely from passion. Her authentic love for fashion became her most effective marketing strategy. Her mother played a vital role by shielding her from negativity, affirming her gifts, and reminding her that passion speaks louder than prejudice.

By staying true to what made her happy, Tammy attracted the right people, those who valued her work, not just her image.

Conclusion: Purpose Doesn't Need Permission

Tammy didn't let judgment define her. She let her work speak for itself. In the face of doubt, she chose to create. And that courage opened doors that led to bigger dreams than she had ever imagined.

Today, Tammy isn't just a designer. She's an inspiration. She employs others, shares her story, and encourages young people with disabilities to believe in their creativity and never give up.

Tammy's story teaches us this: when your purpose is fueled by love, it doesn't matter who doubts you. Keep creating. The right people will see the masterpiece, not the maker's label.

Because true talent doesn't need validation, it just needs the courage to shine.

Conclusion: When Bias Meets Brilliance

The stories of Tina, Lee, and Tammy shine a powerful light on the invisible battles many entrepreneurs face, not from market conditions or lack of skill, but from the biases and prejudices that exist in the hearts of others.

Tina faced racial bias in the professional world, where some clients refused to work with her simply because she was African American. She responded not with anger but with strategy, adapting her approach to ensure her firm could still grow while maintaining her integrity and delivering excellence. Over time, her service broke through stereotypes, and she began to transform perceptions from the inside out.

Lee endured xenophobia during the COVID-19 pandemic. His once-thriving Chinese restaurant became a target of unfair discrimination, threatening the legacy he had built with his family. But through patience, resilience, and adaptation, Lee held on until the tides turned. Now he operates not only with success but with wisdom, ready for the unexpected.

Tammy, a talented young fashion designer with special needs, faced doubts and dismissal from those who judged her by her appearance rather than her artistry. But with the loving support of her mother and a return to the joy of creating, she began to thrive, drawing in customers, landing contracts, and eventually running her own production team. She proved that passion, persistence, and authenticity will always find their audience.

Each story reveals a different face of discrimination, yet they all share the same message: prejudice may close some doors, but purpose has the power to open new ones.

In business and in life, the true test is not whether others believe in you, but whether you believe in yourself enough to keep showing up, creating, and striving in the face of adversity. These entrepreneurs didn't just survive bias. They rose above it, transforming pain into purpose and doubt into undeniable success.

Chapter 14
When It All Falls Apart — And the Technology Keeps Changing

Running a business has never been simple, but today's version of entrepreneurship comes with challenges previous generations could have never imagined. Owning a business is not just a career; it's a lifestyle, a constant mental load, and a responsibility that wakes up with you every morning. People dream of freedom, flexibility, and control, but they rarely see the weight that comes with it. Because the truth is: entrepreneurship is beautiful, but it is also brutally demanding.

And sometimes, just when you think everything is finally stable, life hits you with something that shakes the entire foundation.

When Disaster Shows Up Overnight

Picture this: You arrive at your business ready for a productive day, only to see shattered glass across the floor. Your door has been kicked in. Inventory is missing. Equipment is destroyed. The break-in didn't just damage your storefront, it damaged your peace. Insurance might cover some costs, but insurance can't fix the fear in your gut. It can't buy back the hours you now must spend cleaning, filing claims, finding vendors, and reassuring customers.

Then come the unexpected government penalties, fees, late filings, and compliance notices. Maybe it's a state regulation you didn't know about. Maybe it's a tax deadline you missed because you were too busy keeping the business alive. Suddenly, you're hit with fines that seem designed to punish you for simply not knowing. And for a business already navigating thin margins, a penalty can feel like a knockout punch.

And business doesn't pause just because you're overwhelmed.

When the Tools You Depend On Fail You

Your walk-in freezer goes out during the night, wiping out thousands of dollars in inventory. The POS system crashes during a peak-hour rush, leaving a line of customers impatient and you scrambling to manually write down transactions. A critical piece of machinery breaks down during a job, halting production and causing delays you can't afford.

But now, these failures are happening in a world where everything is digital. The more entrepreneurs rely on technology, the more devastating it is when that technology malfunctions.

Cloud systems go offline. Credit card processors freeze.

Apps update and suddenly stop working. Wi-Fi drops and your entire workflow collapses.

We live in a business environment where even a three-minute outage can cost hundreds or thousands of dollars.

When People Fail You Too

Technology may glitch, but nothing stings like human disappointment.

An employee you trained and invested in walks out without notice. Another one clocks in late, steals time, or worse, steals product or cash. Someone you trusted with keys to your business violates that trust.

These are not petty inconveniences. These are emotional hits that make you question whether you're leading correctly or whether your judgment is flawed.

Even without theft or betrayal, poor attitudes, high turnover, and toxic culture can drain the life out of a business faster than any financial issue. Suddenly, instead of growing your business, you're babysitting adults, settling disputes, covering shifts, retraining new hires, and trying to build a culture that refuses to build itself.

The New Era of Automation, A Blessing and a Threat

Entrepreneurship today is not only about managing people, it's about navigating a world where technology is evolving faster than most small businesses can keep up.

Automation has stepped into industries like a quiet storm.

Walk into stores now and you'll find fewer cashiers and more self-checkout stations.

Restaurants are testing robotic servers.

Some warehouses are replacing the human workforce with automated lifting machines.

Delivery companies are testing drones and driverless vehicles.

Manufacturers are moving toward AI-driven machines that don't call in sick, don't take lunch breaks, and don't need benefits.

For business owners already overwhelmed with staffing challenges, automation seems like the solution they've been dreaming of:

No payroll taxes. No call-outs. No attitudes. No theft. No overtime. No training headaches.

But the flip side? Automation introduces a new category of vulnerabilities that entrepreneurs are not prepared for.

Robots don't notice theft.

AI systems can't recognize human dishonesty or fraud.

Self-checkout machines don't know if a customer skipped an item.

Automated inventory systems can't feel when something seems off.

A robot loading a truck can't tell you that a pallet looks unstable.

Technology can't think critically in a crisis.

Even worse, when automation fails, it fails big. Unlike a human who can adjust, improvise, or communicate, a robot or digital system shuts down without warning, and your entire operation can fall apart with it.

A POS system crash can stop all sales.

A smart freezer malfunction can spoil thousands in food overnight.

AI scheduling tools can glitch and leave you understaffed.

Internet-dependent machinery can halt because of a simple power outage.

The more we embrace technology, the more we must prepare for its shortcomings.

The Modern Entrepreneur's Reality

Entrepreneurship has never been for the faint of heart, but today's landscape demands even more resilience, flexibility, and critical thinking than before.

You must balance:

- People problems
- Technology issues
- Regulatory changes
- Customer expectations
- Digital transitions
- Cybersecurity threats
- Cash flow struggles
- Staffing shortages
- Rising costs
- Supply chain interruptions

This is why so many business owners feel overwhelmed. Not because they're doing something wrong, but because the game has changed, and it keeps changing.

But Even When It All Falls Apart… You Rise

The purpose of this chapter isn't to create fear. It's to remind entrepreneurs that the chaos you're experiencing is real, and you're not alone.

Every system failure, every staffing nightmare, every broken machine, every unexpected bill, every stolen item, every crashed app, every broken freezer, every compliance letter, they are all part of the unfiltered truth of entrepreneurship that nobody warns you about.

But every challenge also sharpens you.

Being an entrepreneur teaches you how to solve problems from angles most people can't see.

It teaches you how to lead under pressure. It teaches you how to stay calm in chaos.

It teaches you patience, grit, and adaptability.

It teaches you how to think ahead, even when time, energy, and resources are depleted.

And most importantly, it teaches you that nothing, not people, not technology, not unexpected loss, can stop a business owner who is committed to finding solutions.

Entrepreneurship Requires Critical Thinking More Than Ever

The purpose of writing this book is to help entrepreneurs strengthen their ability to:

- Think ahead
- Anticipate problems
- Protect their businesses
- Adapt to changing technology
- Build systems that survive chaos
- Strengthen leadership
- Improve decision-making
- And most importantly, keep profits growing

Whether the future brings more automation, more technology, or more challenges, one thing remains the same:

Entrepreneurs who think critically, stay prepared, and embrace change will always survive.

When everything falls apart, your systems, your staff, your equipment, your confidence, that is the moment true entrepreneurs rise. Not because they never fall, but because they learn how to rebuild stronger every time.

Conclusion, When Pressure Builds, Strength Emerges

The truth is, business ownership will always test your limits. Some days, everything feels like it's falling apart, systems glitch, employees disappoint, customers complain, regulators surprise you, and technology evolves faster than you can adapt. These moments can leave you questioning your decisions, your leadership, and your ability to keep going.

But buried inside every breakdown is an invitation, an invitation to evolve.

Entrepreneurship forces you to grow in ways you never expected. You learn to lead through uncertainty. You learn to solve problems before they become crises. You learn to shift with the times, whether that means hiring smarter, automating processes, or building systems with enough protection and backup to withstand the chaos around you.

Most importantly, you learn that your ability to endure has very little to do with what breaks, and everything to do with how you respond.

Technology may advance. Markets may change. Staff may come and go. Systems may fail. But your discipline, your resilience, and your commitment to your vision will always remain your greatest assets.

This chapter wasn't written to highlight the failures, it was written to highlight the strength inside every entrepreneur who keeps showing up despite them. Because when your back is against the wall and everything feels unsteady, that's when real entrepreneurs rise. That's when your creativity sharpens, your instincts strengthen, and your determination becomes unshakable.

In the end, entrepreneurship is not about avoiding problems, it's about mastering them. It's about adapting quickly, protecting your business wisely, and thinking critically in a world where both human behaviors and technology continue to evolve without warning.

The challenges will come. The pressure will come. But so will the growth, the wisdom, and the breakthroughs.

This is the journey. This is the work.

This is the rise that happens when everything falls apart.

And you, like so many business owners who have walked this hard road, are far stronger than you know.

Chapter 15
The Reputation Ripple: Cher's Wake-Up Call

The Story

Cher had spent four years building her professional consulting service, offering everything from administrative support to personal assistance. Her dedication and willingness to go above and beyond earned her a loyal client base and a stellar reputation.

However, as her business grew, Cher became complacent. She began to take her clients for granted, accepting monthly payments while delivering subpar service. Tasks were often delayed until clients complained, and she developed an attitude that her time was more valuable than what her clients were paying.

The turning point came when her largest client requested a meeting. He expressed concerns about the decline in her service quality, stating that she no longer provided the exceptional service she once provided. Instead of listening and addressing his concerns, Cher became irate, yelling that she didn't need his business. The client promptly canceled his services.

This client, with a significant following on social media and a strong presence on review platforms like Yelp, shared his negative experience publicly. His review detailed Cher's unprofessional behavior and the decline in her service quality. The impact was immediate and severe. Existing clients began to question their relationship with Cher, and potential clients were deterred by the negative publicity. Her business suffered a significant downturn.

Realizing the gravity of the situation, Cher took a step back to reflect. She acknowledged her mistakes and reached out to former clients with sincere apologies, taking full responsibility for her actions. She explained that she had lost sight of her commitment to excellence and expressed a genuine desire to make amends.

While not all clients returned, some appreciated her honesty and decided to give her another chance. Cher learned that maintaining a good reputation requires consistent effort and humility. She understood that trust, once broken, takes time and dedication to rebuild.

The Solution

Cher's experience underscores the importance of:

- Consistent Service Quality: Delivering exceptional service should be a continuous effort, not just during the initial stages of client relationships.
- Active Listening: Being receptive to client feedback and addressing concerns promptly can prevent misunderstandings and dissatisfaction.
- Professionalism Under Pressure: Maintaining composure, even when faced with criticism, is crucial. Reacting emotionally can exacerbate the situation.
- Reputation Management: Online reviews significantly influence potential clients. Addressing negative reviews with empathy and a willingness to resolve issues can mitigate damage.
- Continuous Improvement: Regularly assessing and improving service offerings ensures that clients feel valued and receive the quality they expect.

Conclusion

Cher's story serves as a cautionary tale about the dangers of complacency and the importance of maintaining professionalism. In today's digital age, where client experiences can be shared widely and instantly, every interaction counts. Business owners must remain vigilant, consistently delivering value and addressing issues proactively. A strong reputation is built over time but can be tarnished quickly. By prioritizing client satisfaction and embracing feedback, businesses can foster trust and ensure long-term success.

"The Cost of Delegation Without Oversight: Dan's Story"

The Story

Dan owned a reputable auto body shop in a tight-knit town where word-of-mouth was the lifeblood of business. Known for his honesty and quality workmanship, Dan had built a loyal customer base over the years. To focus on expanding his business, he hired a new mechanic, Mike, and promoted him to manager, entrusting him with daily operations.

Initially, things seemed to run smoothly. However, Dan noticed a decline in repeat business and fewer referrals. Unbeknownst to him, Mike had been engaging in unethical practices: upselling unnecessary parts and services, overcharging customers, and treating them rudely. One incident involved a customer who came in for a simple brake job and oil change. After the service, the car made unusual noises. When the customer returned, Mike insisted it would cost an additional $1,500 to fix the issue. Suspicious, the customer sought a second opinion and discovered that Mike had deliberately tampered with the vehicle to create additional problems.

The disgruntled customer posted a scathing review online, accusing the shop of fraudulent practices. This review gained traction, leading to a cascade of negative publicity. Dan, shocked by the revelations, confronted Mike and terminated his employment. Upon further investigation, Dan found that several long-time clients had been overcharged. He reached out to them, offered sincere apologies, and provided refunds. Despite his efforts, the damage to his shop's reputation was significant, and rebuilding trust proved challenging.

The Solution

Dan's experience underscores the importance of active oversight and maintaining ethical standards in business operations. To address the fallout and prevent future issues, Dan implemented several key strategies:

1. Reinstated Direct Oversight: Dan resumed a hands-on approach to daily operations, ensuring that all services met his established standards of quality and integrity.
2. Established Clear Protocols: He developed comprehensive guidelines for customer interactions, service procedures, and billing practices to ensure consistency and transparency.
3. Enhanced Staff Training: Dan invested in regular training sessions focusing on customer service, ethical practices, and technical skills to foster a culture of professionalism.
4. Implemented Feedback Mechanisms: He introduced a system for customers to provide feedback directly, allowing for prompt identification and resolution of issues.
5. Proactive Reputation Management: Dan actively monitored online reviews and responded to feedback, demonstrating his commitment to customer satisfaction and continuous improvement.

Conclusion

Dan's story serves as a cautionary tale about the risks of delegating critical responsibilities without proper oversight. In service-based industries, a single employee's misconduct can tarnish a hard-earned reputation. Business owners must remain vigilant, uphold ethical standards, and foster a culture of accountability. By taking swift corrective actions and prioritizing customer trust, it's possible to recover from setbacks and rebuild a reputable brand.

"The Chemical Wake-Up Call: Cindy's Salon Crisis"

The Story

Cindy owned a thriving beauty salon offering a wide range of services, including hair styling, nail care, eyebrow treatments, pedicures, and massages. Her commitment to excellence attracted a loyal clientele who trusted her expertise.

One day, a regular client visited the salon for an eyebrow tint. As Cindy applied the tinting solution, the client began to experience a severe allergic reaction. Her skin became irritated, and swelling occurred around the treated area. Cindy immediately removed the product and provided first aid, but the client's condition necessitated medical attention. The client later informed Cindy of her intention to file a lawsuit.

Though the claim was processed through Cindy's workers' compensation insurance, sparing her significant financial loss, the incident served as a stark reminder of the potential risks associated with salon services. Cindy realized that, despite her experience, she had not implemented adequate measures to prevent such occurrences.

The Solution

Determined to prevent future incidents and protect her clients and business, Cindy took several proactive steps:

1. Implementation of Detailed Consent Forms: Cindy introduced comprehensive consent forms for all services involving chemicals. These forms included detailed information about the products used, potential risks, and required clients to disclose any known allergies or sensitivities.
2. Mandatory Patch Testing: For services involving chemical applications, Cindy instituted mandatory patch tests at least 24 hours before the scheduled appointment to identify potential allergic reactions.
3. Staff Training and Protocols: Cindy conducted training sessions for her staff to ensure they understood the importance of client consultations, proper application techniques, and emergency response procedures.
4. Transparent Communication: Cindy updated her salon's policies to emphasize transparency, ensuring clients were fully informed about the procedures and products used.
5. Client Relations and Reputation Management: Recognizing the importance of maintaining trust, Cindy personally reached out to the affected client to apologize and offered complimentary services as a gesture of goodwill. She also addressed the incident publicly, reinforcing her commitment to client safety and satisfaction.

Conclusion

Cindy's experience underscores the critical importance of proactive risk management in the beauty industry. By implementing thorough consultation processes, obtaining informed consent, and maintaining open communication, salon owners can safeguard their clients' well-being and their business's reputation. Cindy's swift and comprehensive response not only mitigated the immediate crisis but also strengthened her salon's commitment to excellence and client care.

The stories of Cher, Dan, and Cindy each illuminate a critical truth in business: success is not built solely on initial effort but sustained by consistent integrity, attentive leadership, and proactive risk management. While their industries differ, their experiences converge on the importance of maintaining trust and accountability.

Cher's journey underscores the dangers of complacency. Her initial dedication to exceptional service waned over time, leading to a decline in client satisfaction and, ultimately, a tarnished reputation. It wasn't until she faced significant client loss that she recognized the need to recommit to her foundational values and rebuild trust.

Dan's experience highlights the risks of delegation without proper oversight. By entrusting his business operations to a manager without adequate supervision, he inadvertently allowed unethical practices to flourish, damaging long-standing customer relationships. His proactive steps to rectify the situation, including client reimbursements and policy overhauls, were essential in restoring his business's integrity.

Cindy's incident reveals the importance of anticipating potential risks and implementing safeguards. An unforeseen allergic reaction from a client prompted her to establish comprehensive consent forms and transparent communication about product ingredients, thereby enhancing client safety and trust.

Collectively, these narratives serve as a compelling reminder that:

- Consistency in Service: Ongoing commitment to quality is vital for sustaining client relationships.

- Effective Oversight: Delegation requires continuous monitoring to ensure alignment with business values.
- Proactive Risk Management: Anticipating potential issues and establishing clear protocols can prevent crises.

In the dynamic landscape of entrepreneurship, vigilance, adaptability, and a steadfast commitment to ethical practices are the cornerstones of enduring success.

Chapter 16
When the Passion Fades

Sheila had built her accounting firm from the ground up. With years of dedication, late nights, client handholding, and a relentless pursuit of excellence, she created a reputation for integrity, fairness, and quality. Her pricing was always competitive, her services consistent, and her impact undeniable. By the time she reached her five-year milestone, her firm was stable, respected, and profitable.

But Sheila wasn't content with just stability, she wanted growth. So, for the first time, she created a marketing budget, $2,000 a month strictly for exposure and client acquisition. That decision opened doors. Leads increased, her brand became more recognized, and her revenue climbed. There were still challenges, of course, demanding clients, tax season chaos, and back-office struggles, but overall, the business was blossoming.

However, when Sheila hit the ten-year mark, something unexpected happened. The passion began to fade. She found herself staring at her office walls with a sense of disconnect. Her health was being tested, high stress, poor sleep, and emotional fatigue. Vacations became more frequent, not as luxuries but as necessities to keep herself from burning out. The more she distanced herself from the office, the more she questioned her purpose in business.

This inner turmoil didn't stem from failure, Sheila was blessed. Her firm allowed her to serve within her faith, support her family, and enjoy financial freedom. Yet, she began to feel guilty for wanting to step away from what God had clearly blessed her with. Was she being ungrateful? Was she throwing away His provision?

Conflicted, Sheila did what many business owners struggle to do, she spoke up. She called a staff meeting, sat down with her team, and vulnerably shared how she was feeling. She expressed her mental and emotional exhaustion, her need to rekindle joy, and her desire to restructure her role so she could step back without shutting the doors.

Her team listened with care and responded with loyalty.

One manager proposed revisiting the pricing model, especially for clients with small monthly packages. These clients were high maintenance but low revenue, burning time and resources disproportionately. The solution? Raise the rates for those packages in a way that would either increase income or naturally phase out those clients.

With Sheila's approval, the pricing changes were sent out by email.

Surprisingly, none of the small clients left. They all accepted the new rates.

Encouraged, the team applied the same strategy to mid-tier clients. Again, no pushbacks. Then the larger clients. The result was the same, full acceptance.

It was a turning point.

The message was loud and clear: Your clients value you, Sheila. You've done a good job, and they see it.

Her office manager later sat down with her and said something that shifted her perspective:

"You're not tired of the business, Sheila, you're tired of how it's been structured. It's time to let the business serve you the way you've served it."

Solution: Reclaiming Ownership and Joy

Sheila began reimagining her business around her life, not the other way around.

Here's how she and her team rebuild her business model for longevity and fulfillment:

Delegated Leadership: Sheila appointed a trusted senior manager to oversee day-to-day operations, empowering the team to make key decisions without her daily input.

Client Tiering: The firm categorizes clients by revenue and engagement level, setting clear boundaries around time and access. High-demand clients require premium pricing or VIP packages.

Selective Client Onboarding: New clients were evaluated through a fit-and-value assessment. If they didn't align with the firm's vision or profitability model, they were respectfully declined.

Reduced Office Time: Sheila created a hybrid schedule for herself, working part-time remotely and only visiting the office for strategic meetings or key planning sessions.

Revived Purpose Projects: She used her new time to mentor young entrepreneurs, create educational content, and contribute more within her faith community, activities that filled her with purpose again.

Self-Care Non-Negotiables: Vacations, wellness routines, and downtime were no longer occasional indulgences; they became scheduled priorities.

Conclusion

What Sheila learned, and what so many entrepreneurs eventually face, is that building a business doesn't mean becoming a prisoner to it. Success is not measured by how much you sacrifice but by how well your business supports your life. After ten years of building, Sheila had earned the right to restructure and realign.

And in doing so, she didn't lose her business, she rediscovered herself.

When the Spark Fades

Story:

Tim was the proud owner of a thriving slicing business that served nearly every major cable provider across the state. His company had built a solid reputation, backed by exceptional reviews and a team of skilled, loyal employees. For years, Tim found purpose and excitement in every job, every new contract, and every satisfied customer. He had built something meaningful from the ground up, something that once gave him tremendous pride.

But something shifted.

As the company grew, so did the weight on his shoulders. Tim started to feel disconnected, fatigued, and unmotivated. The excitement that once drove him began to feel like a burden. He started contemplating stepping away from the business entirely. Concerned about his mental state, he opened up to his brother during a late-night phone call.

His brother, deeply empathetic and concerned, encouraged Tim to take a break. "Step back for a while and clear your mind," he said. "I'll hold things down with your team until you figure out your next move." With hesitation but relief, Tim accepted the offer and took a much-needed two-week vacation.

During Tim's absence, his brother stepped in seamlessly. He empowered the managers by giving them more responsibilities and compensated them fairly for the extra workload. The business didn't just survive, it ran efficiently. But when the two weeks passed and Tim didn't return, his brother grew worried.

Two months went by with no words from Tim. He wasn't answering calls or texts. Finally, desperate to check on him, his brother drove to his house. What he found was alarming. Tim was still in bed, withdrawn, and the house was in disarray. It was clear: Tim was in the depths of depression.

His brother refused to walk away. He gently but firmly pulled Tim out of bed, brewed some coffee, and they talked for hours. That moment became the turning point. Tim's brother urged him to seek professional help, and together they found a therapist. He also arranged for a cleaning service to help get the house back in order, knowing that a clean space often brings mental clarity.

Solution:

With his brother's support, Tim began the journey to recover. His brother continued running the business while Tim focused on his mental health. Over the course of the next few months, Tim slowly began to re-engage, first through small meetings, then handling a few projects a week. He realized that the joy he once had wasn't gone, it had just been buried beneath years of stress and exhaustion.

Rather than returning to his former full-time grind, Tim made a conscious decision to restructure his role. He worked only on select days and delegated larger operational decisions to his trusted managers. He also brought his brother on board as a permanent partner, giving him a formal role in the company.

This shift allowed Tim to remain involved without sacrificing his well-being.

Conclusion:

Tim's story is a reminder that success without balance can become a silent burden. Burnout doesn't always look like failure; it can hide behind glowing reviews and a busy calendar. Sometimes, the strongest thing a business owner can do is ask for help.

Through vulnerability, family support, and structural change, Tim not only protected his business but reclaimed his peace of mind. He now leads with a new perspective, one where delegation is a strength, balance is necessary, and joy is non-negotiable.

Let Tim's journey serve as a lesson: If you lose your joy in the business you built, it's not the end, it's a signal that it's time to reset, realign, and renew.

A Business Too Heavy to Hold Alone

Story:

Mimi had spent over a decade building a thriving beauty supply store that became a staple in her community. From the trendiest hair products to retail handbags and specialty beauty items, her store offered it all. With over ten employees and a CPA managing the finances, on paper, Mimi created a successful and sustainable business.

But behind the scenes, Mimi was exhausted.

She hadn't taken a real vacation in 15 years. Her life had revolved around the business from day one. She had weathered theft, employee conflicts, and even workplace drama sparked by romantic relationships among staff. Despite the challenges, Mimi held it together with strength and grace, but at a cost.

After 11 years of giving everything to the store, she felt depleted. The passion she once had for the business was gone. Mimi confessed to her husband that she was thinking of selling the business altogether. "I just want peace. I want time with my family. I want a break," she said with tears in her eyes.

Her husband, though concerned, responded with practical hesitation. "This store is our bread and butter. What will we do if you walk away?" Mimi explained that it wasn't just about the store anymore, it was about her well-being. After some back and forth, they reached a compromise: he would hire a new manager, and they would take a much-needed vacation together.

Mimi personally trained the new manager, ensuring she understood the business operations. Then she informed her team she would be traveling abroad for two weeks and would have limited phone access. It was the first time in years that Mimi allowed herself to breathe.

But the relief was short-lived.

Upon returning, Mimi stopped by the store and was shocked by the chaos. The line of customers stretched around the block, and only two overwhelmed staff members were working. Worse, two of her longest-standing employees, trusted team members who had been with her from the beginning, quit.

She jumped in to help, quickly restoring order, and then pulled the new manager aside for answers. The manager admitted that the two key employees left because they disagreed with her management style and abrupt changes. Mimi immediately called both former employees, apologized, and asked them to return. Thankfully, they did.

Solution:

Mimi realized something critical: the business needed trusted leadership, but it didn't have to be her alone. She sat down with her two best employees and had an honest conversation. She told them, "My job is gone. I either need your help running this store, or I'm going to sell it."

To her surprise, they not only understood, they offered their full support. Mimi offered them a minority stake in the business in exchange for stepping into leadership roles. The idea of ownership excited them, and they eagerly agreed.

Together, they began restructuring. They hired new staff, improved training protocols, and delegated operations. Mimi reduced her time in the store to just three days a week. The store didn't just survive, it thrived. With her most loyal employees now invested in the business's success, things operated better than ever.

Conclusion:

Mimi's journey speaks to a common truth among long-time business owners: burnout doesn't always come from failure, it often comes from success carried alone for too long.

By shifting her mindset from doing it all to leading with support, Mimi created a new chapter not just for her business, but for herself. She found balance, relief, and, unexpectedly, two trusted partners and friends who helped reignite the passion she thought was gone for good.

Mimi learned that letting go doesn't mean giving up, it means making room for something better.

Learning to Let Go Without Giving Up

Each of the stories in this chapter reveals a hard truth that many entrepreneurs eventually face but few are prepared for: burnout is real, and it can hit even the most passionate, driven business owners.

Sheila, Tim, and Mimi were all deeply committed to the businesses they built from the ground up. Their hard work, sacrifices, and resilience led to growth, success, and community impact. But behind the scenes, the daily grind, constant pressure, and emotional toll wore them down. They each reached a point where the business they once loved felt like a burden.

Their stories follow a common thread, the courage to admit when enough is enough and the wisdom to seek help rather than walk away entirely. Whether it was taking a vacation, restructuring leadership, delegating responsibilities, or bringing in trusted team members and family, they all found a way to keep the business moving forward while protecting their health, joy, and peace of mind.

The lesson here is powerful:

You don't have to carry it all to be successful. You don't have to lose yourself to keep your business alive.

True leadership is not just about pushing harder, it's about creating systems, empowering others, and knowing when to step back so that you can show up stronger.

For every entrepreneur reading this, know that stepping away doesn't mean failure. Sometimes, it's the smartest business move you can make. Prioritize your wellness, protect your peace, and never be afraid to ask for support. Your business can still grow, even if you're not at the center of it every day.

Chapter 17
Building on Broken Foundations

Larry was a talented contractor with a reputation for getting things done fast and done right. His construction cleanup and property restoration business served developers, banks, and real estate investors who trusted him for quick turnarounds. Demand was high, and Larry's crew stayed busy.

But while Larry knew how to run a job site, he never learned how to run the business behind the job site.

To "keep things simple," he paid all his workers in cash. No W-9s. No 1099s. No payroll system. No records, just envelopes of money handed out on Fridays. He bought his supplies the same way, paying cash and tossing the receipts into a drawer to "deal with at tax time."

His clients paid him by check, which he deposited into his business account. But as soon as the money hit, he withdrew large amounts of cash to pay workers and buy materials. To Larry, this felt normal. It was how he had always operated. He didn't see the danger.

Then came the moment every growing entrepreneur eventually faces:

he needed money to scale.

Larry wanted to expand his team, buy additional equipment, and take on bigger contracts. To make that happen, he applied for a business loan. That is when everything unraveled.

The bank asked for the basics, profit and loss statements, tax returns, payroll records, and financial documentation.

Larry had none.

Scrambling, he hired an accountant to prepare the paperwork. But the accountant quickly discovered the problem: there was no documentation to support Larry's income, expenses, or payroll. There were no subcontractor agreements, no payment logs, no time sheets, and no traceable contractor records.

When the accountant asked how much he paid his workers, Larry told him,

"Just put down what I tell you."

The accountant refused. Without proof, those numbers couldn't legally be used.

Desperate, Larry reached out to former workers to confirm payments. Most refused. Some worried about their own taxes. Others had moved on and didn't want involvement. A few flat-out denied ever being paid.

With almost no documentation, the accountant had no choice but to report the income without matching expenses or deductions.

Larry was hit with a large tax bill.

And with his finances incomplete and unverifiable, the bank denied his loan.

His entire plan for growth collapsed because the business he built had no foundation.

Business Lessons

What Larry's Story Teaches Every Business Owner

1. If you can't prove it, it doesn't exist.
2. In business, undocumented expenses and unreported payroll leave you exposed financially and legally.
3. Cash-only systems create invisible businesses.
4. Banks, lenders, and investors cannot work with assumptions or verbal explanations. They need records.
5. Worker classification matters.
6. Paying people as "contractors" without forms or documentation can trigger tax problems, audits, and penalties.
7. Financial structure is not optional. It is required for growth.
8. Clean records, proper payroll, and organized books are part of running a legitimate business, not extra tasks you "get to later."
9. You can't scale what you can't track.
10. Bigger contracts require transparency. Without proper financials, you cannot qualify for funding or expansion opportunities.
11. Good bookkeeping protects profit.
12. Tracking receipts, using accounting software, and following compliance rules help reduce taxes, avoid errors, and create financial stability.

Conclusion

Larry's story is a warning to every business owner operating on trust, cash, and habit. What feels easy in the moment often becomes incredibly costly later. When it's time to grow, apply for funding, or take on bigger opportunities, only one thing matters:

your numbers must be documented, accurate, and verifiable.

A business built on cash and guesswork may survive for a while, but it cannot thrive in the long term. The foundation will eventually crack.

The truth is simple:

Strong businesses are built on strong records.

Proper documentation isn't just about taxes, it's about credibility, stability, and peace of mind. Whether you're starting out or scaling up, the systems you put in place today will determine what opportunities you qualify for tomorrow.

Lesson Learned:

Never build your business on a foundation that cannot be proven. Good records protect your growth, your reputation, and your future.

Part Two

When Life Demands Proof

Lisa was a gifted hairstylist who lived a simple, peaceful life. She rented a small private suite inside a local salon where she worked by appointment only, styling loyal clients who adored her work. She had no children, shared a home with her mother, and kept her expenses low. Her world was uncomplicated, and her business ran entirely on cash.

Lisa never tracked her income. She didn't keep receipts, report her earnings, or file taxes. To her, it wasn't necessary, she always had enough to pay her bills, and her chair was consistently booked. As far as she was concerned, life was steady and secure.

Until the day everything changed.

While finishing up a client's blowout, Lisa received a phone call that shattered her world, her mother had been killed in a sudden accident. Grief consumed her. She was thrust into responsibilities she had never imagined: funeral arrangements, legal paperwork, estate matters, and the emotional burden of losing the one person she depended on most.

But the challenges didn't stop there.

When she returned to the salon to pick up her schedule, she found a 30-day notice taped to her studio door. Her rental agreement was expiring, and the landlord required proof of income and tax returns to renew her lease. He explained that going forward, all tenants had to show they earned at least three times the rent.

Lisa froze. She had no pay stubs.

No tax filings. No profit and loss statement. No documented income at all.

Just a full roster of clients, and no way to prove her earnings.

She tried to explain her situation, but business decisions require documentation, not verbal explanations. Emotion couldn't replace verification.

Feeling lost, Lisa confided in a long-time client who had always admired her work ethic. Moved by her story, the client stepped in to help. She provided temporary pay stubs through her own business so Lisa wouldn't immediately lose her space. Then she insisted Lisa meet with a professional accountant to finally organize her financial life.

Those pay stubs bought her time, but not a future.

Lisa took the advice seriously. She hired the accountant, committed to rebuilding her financial structure, and began transforming her cash-based hustle into a real business.

Business Lessons

What Lisa's Story Teaches Every Entrepreneur

1. Cash-only income creates invisible earnings.
2. If your money isn't documented, it doesn't count when you need it, whether for housing, loans, grants, or emergencies.
3. Life changes fast, and documentation protects you.
4. When unexpected events occur, proper financial records allow you to make decisions from a place of stability rather than crisis.
5. Professional support creates credibility.
6. A good accountant doesn't just file taxes, they help build the financial history lenders and landlords require.
7. Your business needs a paper trail.
8. Tracking appointments, payments, and expenses isn't extra work, it's essential proof of your income and professionalism.
9. Personal and business finances must be separate.
10. A dedicated business account builds clarity, legitimacy, and financial structure.
11. Compliance is not optional.
12. Tax returns, profit and loss statements, and organized records are required for nearly every major adult responsibility, including housing.
13. What you can't prove, you can't use.
14. Income that isn't documented cannot support you when life demands verification.

Conclusion

Lisa's story is one that many cash-based business owners, especially in beauty, wellness, and service industries, can deeply relate to. When everything is going well, it's easy to ignore paperwork, taxes, and tracking systems. But life can change in an instant, and when it does, the world doesn't accept verbal explanations or loyal clientele as proof of income.

Documentation is security. Structure is protection. Compliance is empowerment.

Lisa learned that if you cannot prove your income, you do not truly own it in the eyes of landlords, lenders, or the law. Her experience serves as a powerful reminder that building a legitimate business isn't just about serving clients, it's about preparing for the unexpected and creating a foundation that supports your future, no matter what life brings.

Part Three

Love, Liquor, and Ledgers

Tim was known far and wide as the man who could turn any event into an unforgettable experience. As a traveling bartender with flawless charm and expert mixology skills, he worked weddings, rooftop parties, corporate galas, high-end private events, and even filled in for restaurants when their bartenders went on vacation. His calendar stayed booked, and his reputation kept him in constant demand.

But behind the vibrant personality and the packed schedule was a business built on one rule:

Cash only. No checks. No bank deposits. No invoices. No paper trails.

Tim loved the freedom of it. No questions. No taxes. No responsibilities. Every weekend brought new events, new tips, and new opportunities for flashy outfits, spontaneous trips, and guilt-free spending.

It was the perfect setup, until love required him to grow up.

At a rooftop event one warm summer night, Tim met Latrice, a graceful, confident nurse with a radiant smile and a structured life. They clicked instantly. Their conversations flowed effortlessly, their chemistry was undeniable, and despite living in different states, they talked every day. As the months passed, their weekend trips turned into something serious.

During one getaway, Latrice asked a simple but life-changing question:

“What are your plans for us?”

Tim didn’t hesitate. He wanted something real, a committed relationship, family introductions, a shared future. He even encouraged her to move to his state so they could start building a life together.

But when the conversation shifted to the practical things, finances, housing, long-term planning, everything stopped.

Latrice, who owned a home, carried good credit, and maintained a well-documented financial life, asked Tim to show his income. Not the cash in his pocket or the list of events he worked, but actual documentation:

- Bank statements
- Tax filings
- Verifiable income
- Business records

Tim proudly pulled out his handwritten list of clients and weekly earnings.

Latrice shook her head gently.

"Baby, this can't get us a house. We can't build a future on money you can't prove."

Tim was stunned. He had never been challenged like this before. In his world, cash was king. But in the real world, banks, lenders, mortgages, and long-term goals, cash with no trail meant nothing.

And he knew he couldn't lose her.

Determined, Tim hired a reputable accountant and made the decision every cash-based entrepreneur eventually faces:

he transitioned from a hustle to a legitimate business.

Business Lessons

What Tim's Story Teaches Every Entrepreneur

1. Cash-based success is fragile.
2. If your income isn't documented, it doesn't count when you need it, for loans, housing, credit, or financial partnerships.
3. Love and life require proof.
4. Relationships, marriages, and shared futures depend on financial transparency. Undocumented earnings can't build a household.
5. Professional structure creates opportunity.
6. Registering your business, keeping records, and filing taxes aren't limitations, they unlock access to funding, growth, and stability.
7. A business is only real when the numbers are real.

8. Invoices, payment records, tax filings, and bank statements are the foundation of financial credibility.
9. Payroll builds your financial identity.
10. Paying yourself a salary gives you verifiable income, necessary for mortgages, loans, and adult responsibilities.
11. You cannot scale on secrecy.
12. Cash hustles keep you working event to event. A legitimate business helps you build assets, hire help, and grow beyond yourself.
13. Compliance protects your future.
14. Operating legally keeps you out of trouble and positions you for long-term success, both personally and professionally.

Conclusion

Tim's journey is a powerful reminder that financial freedom without financial structure is a temporary illusion. Operating strictly in cash may feel liberating, but it creates invisible income, denies you access to opportunities, and limits your ability to build a life with someone else.

Real love, real business, and real success all require documentation, transparency, and structure.

By becoming compliant, Tim didn't just save his relationship, he transformed his entire future. His business blossomed, his credibility increased, and he finally gained the stability needed to build a home and a family.

Lesson Learned:

If you want to build something lasting, whether it's a business or a relationship, you must create a foundation that is real, visible, and verifiable. Don't wait until life or love demands proof. Build your structure now so your success can stand tomorrow.

The Price of Being Off the Record

In each of these stories, Larry, Lisa, and Tim, we meet hardworking, talented entrepreneurs who built successful businesses with skill, passion, and dedication. Yet all three found themselves in crisis the moment life demanded something they could not produce:

Proof.

Larry couldn't secure financing because his cash-based system left no paper trail.

Lisa couldn't renew her rental space because she had no documented income.

Tim couldn't move forward in love because his financial habits couldn't support a future.

Their issue wasn't a lack of effort, talent, or opportunity, it was a lack of structure.

Many cash-based entrepreneurs believe that operating "off the record" is freedom. No tracking. No taxes. No paperwork. But as these stories show, freedom is temporary and expensive.

When it's time to get a loan, apply for housing, buy a home, protect your business, or build a future, only documented income counts. Paper trails, not handshakes, open doors.

Each of these entrepreneurs eventually discovered a painful truth:

If you can't prove your income, you don't truly own it.

Larry learned it when the bank said no.

Lisa learned it when life's hardest moment collided with financial reality.

Tim learned it when love demanded accountability.

And once they embraced structure, bookkeeping, documentation, tax compliance, and financial systems, their entire lives and businesses changed. They didn't just recover, they elevated.

Their success didn't come from starting over. It came from getting organized.

Business Lessons

What Every Entrepreneur Must Take Away

1. Track Every Dollar
2. Income and expenses must be documented. What you record is what you can deduct, defend, or use to grow your business.
3. Report and Pay Your Taxes
4. Compliance builds credibility. It is the foundation lenders, landlords, and financial institutions rely on.
5. Keep Business and Personal Finances Separate
6. Separate bank accounts, organized bookkeeping, and verifiable payroll protect your business and strengthen your financial identity.
7. Invest in a Professional
8. A skilled accountant is not an expense, it is an asset. They help you build structure, prepare for the future, and stay protected.
9. Cash Isn't the Enemy, Lack of Documentation Is
10. You can earn in cash, but you must track it. Income that isn't recorded doesn't count when you need it most.

Conclusion

Operating off the record may feel convenient, but it creates invisible income, hidden risks, and missed opportunities. Your business is only as strong as the system behind it.

Shine a light on your finances. Document your success. Build with structure, not guesswork.

When you bring your business into the light, the opportunities you once thought were out of reach become achievable and sustainable.

Chapter 18
The Price of Disregard

Sam was the kind of entrepreneur who never stopped moving. He ran a busy grocery store that served the community and owned two smaller businesses on the side. In total, more than 25 employees worked under his umbrella of operations. And while Sam was ambitious and hardworking, everything functioned as well as it did because of one person at the center of his administrative world, his accountant.

She wasn't just a CPA who balanced his books. She was his silent backbone.

She handled payroll, HR issues, employee onboarding, compliance filings, annual updates, policy revisions, internal conflicts, and any situation that required professionalism or protection. She made sure Sam stayed out of legal trouble, kept the staff aligned, and maintained order behind the scenes. She stepped in during emergencies, corrected internal mistakes, educated Sam's managers, and routinely did more than she was ever paid to do, simply because she cared.

But Sam didn't see any of that.

To him, paying an invoice meant he didn't owe gratitude. He assumed every task, no matter how big, stressful, or unexpected, was just "part of the job." He rarely thanked her. He never acknowledged her team's effort. He didn't ask questions, didn't check in, and didn't see the amount of labor being carried quietly on his behalf.

And then, everything shifted. A Breaking Point Hidden in Plain Sight

One afternoon, a serious employee complaint landed on the accountant's desk. A manager had been accused of mistreatment, and legally, the issue required immediate action.

The accountant handled it swiftly and professionally, interviewing staff, documenting facts, updating Sam, and making sure the business stayed compliant with labor laws. It was a situation that could have easily escalated into a lawsuit or state investigation, but she resolved it with precision and care.

Instead of appreciating the protection she had just provided, Sam snapped.

He blamed her for not preventing the issue in the first place. He publicly criticized her staff. He dismissed their professionalism and belittled the very people who had kept his businesses safe for years.

For the CPA, that was the final line.

She requested a private meeting and, with calm professionalism, explained that their firm would be withdrawing services. She provided 30 days for Sam to transition. No arguments. No negotiations.

Sam froze. He didn't expect her to walk away.

He tried to apologize, but it wasn't enough. The trust was gone, and her team was exhausted from years of carrying more weight than they received credit for.

And so she left. Reality Arrives Quietly, Then Loudly

At first, Sam brushed it off. "An accountant is an accountant," he told himself. Numbers are numbers. Anyone could do this.

He hired a new firm and expected life to go on as usual.

But within months, everything fell apart.

Employee issues weren't being handled or documented.

Policies lapsed. HR conflicts were ignored. Compliance deadlines were missed.

Financial reports were delayed. Managers were confused.

The smooth workflow he once enjoyed became chaotic.

Only then did Sam realize:

The CPA hadn't just been doing her job; she had been doing everyone's job.

She was his protection, his order, his compliance, his structure, his unspoken foundation.

He just never saw it.

A Humble Return

Humbled and frustrated with the growing problems, Sam reached out, not with excuses, but with honesty.

He apologized for not appreciating her.

He acknowledged everything she used to handle.

He admitted that running his businesses without her oversight had opened his eyes.

He offered a new contract with higher compensation, but more importantly, he promised respect.

After careful thought, the CPA agreed to return, but only under her terms. Boundaries were set. Expectations were clear. Respect was non-negotiable.

And Sam changed.

He included her in strategic decisions.

He thanked her team publicly.

He encouraged his managers to treat her office as an essential part of operations, not an afterthought.

This time, Sam truly understood the value of professional loyalty.

Business Lessons

What Every Business Owner Must Take Away

1. Your Support Team Is Part of Your Foundation
2. Professionals behind the scenes, CPAs, HR reps, administrators, consultants, keep your business compliant, protected, and functioning smoothly. They carry weight you may never see.
3. Respect Is Not Optional
4. Paying for a service doesn't replace appreciation. When people feel undervalued, they eventually leave, and the cost of replacing them is always higher than the cost of respecting them.
5. The Invisible Work Is the Most Valuable
6. Compliance tasks, documentation, employee management, and policy creation may not generate profit directly, but they prevent lawsuits, penalties, shutdowns, and chaos.

7. A Skilled Advisor Is Not "Replaceable."
8. Anyone can produce numbers.
9. Not everyone can understand your operations, protect your business, and carry the responsibilities that keep you out of legal trouble.
10. Culture Starts at the Top
11. If a business owner disrespects advisors, employees will follow. Appreciation must be modeled consistently.

Conclusion

The Moment You Stop Appreciating Your Team, You Start Losing Them

Sam's story is a warning for every entrepreneur: the strength of your business isn't just in your products or your revenue, it's in the people who keep the machine running.

Your advisors, bookkeepers, CPAs, HR support, and administrative staff may not stand in the spotlight, but they are the backbone of your success. When you fail to appreciate them, you risk losing the very stability that allows your business to thrive.

Never wait until someone is gone to acknowledge their worth.

Honor the people who keep your business afloat, because without them, even the strongest company can crumble.

Part Two

The Cost of Chasing Promises

Ellen had spent years building a successful marketing agency. With nine highly skilled professionals, a roster of well-known clients, and a reputation for delivering bold, effective campaigns, her business was thriving. But what truly kept everything running smoothly was the structure behind the scenes, her reliable CPA and her trusted attorney. They managed her compliance, reviewed contracts, protected her financially, and ensured everything stayed in order.

Then one weekend, a simple dinner conversation shifted everything.

While visiting a longtime friend in another state, who also happened to be a CPA, Ellen listened as her friend proudly shared how she helped her clients scale at a rapid speed. She spoke about tripling revenues, restructuring companies, and "taking businesses to the next level in months, not years."

The confidence was intoxicating. The promises were compelling.

And Ellen found herself imagining what her own company could become.

Inspired, she asked her friend if she would take over her accounting and financial strategy. Her friend eagerly agreed.

The next day, driven by excitement, Ellen called her current CPA and announced the transition. She asked that all records, backups, and access be transferred immediately. The CPA handled the switch professionally and respectfully, exactly as she always had.

But within three months, Ellen realized something was wrong.

The detailed monthly financial statements she once depended on never arrived. Emails went unanswered. Questions were brushed off with vague responses. Her old CPA used to proactively flag issues, analyze trends, and offer strategic guidance, but now, silence filled the gaps where support used to be.

When Ellen confronted her friend, she received apologies and a promise to send the reports “right away.”

The next morning, the reports arrived, but they were different. Unclear. Missing information. Not aligned with her prior structure. Confused, she asked for an explanation.

And the truth came out.

The new firm used an entirely different accounting system. Instead of importing her years of historical data, data her original CPA had carefully built, they had only entered opening balances and tried to reconstruct the rest. Years of financial history had been erased, replaced with estimates.

Her friend reassured her that it would just take more time to “learn her business” and “analyze trends.” Ellen reminded her:

“You said my revenue would increase in the first quarter.”

Again, more apologies. More promises. Hoping things would improve, Ellen waited.

Two months later, nothing had changed. Reports were vague.

The outsourced bookkeeper handling her account didn’t know her company.

Basic questions couldn’t be answered.

Most of the work had been sent overseas to cut costs, and communication was scattered.

Her business was still profitable, but Ellen felt unsupported and misled.

Desperate for clarity, she flew back to meet her friend. She laid everything on the table:

"How is my business really performing?"

"What do I need to cut?"

"What should I change?"

"What steps will increase revenue?"

Her friend had no concrete answers. Only excuses. Only more time is needed.

And that's when Ellen finally saw the truth, she had traded a strategic partner for a personality.

She had abandoned excellence for excitement. She had confused confidence with competence.

Humbled, she reached out to her former CPA, hoping to restore their partnership.

But her old accountant had already onboarded a larger client and no longer had the capacity to take her back.

The partnership Ellen walked away from could not be recovered.

Business Lessons

What Ellen's Experience Teaches Every Entrepreneur

1. A good advisor is worth more than a good pitch.
2. Promises mean nothing without consistent delivery. Real value is found in clarity, communication, and reliability.
3. Historical knowledge cannot be replaced.

4. Years of financial understanding guide strategic decisions. Starting over isn't just inconvenient, it is costly.
5. Don't confuse excitement with improvement.
6. Big promises can cloud judgment. Growth requires structure, not hype.
7. Friendship doesn't equal competence.
8. Personal comfort does not guarantee professional capability. Your business deserves expertise, not familiarity.
9. Change should be intentional, not emotional.
10. Switch advisors because you've outgrown them or lack support, not because someone sounded confident over dinner.
11. Loyalty is earned over time, don't abandon it lightly.
12. A partner who shows up consistently, asks the right questions, and protects your business is worth keeping.

Conclusion

Ellen's story is a reminder that in business, not all help is helpful. The loudest person in the room isn't always the most skilled, and the most confident promises rarely replace proven performance. Strategic decisions must be rooted in facts, results, and clarity, not emotion, pressure, or excitement.

The professionals who understand your business, guide you with honesty, and deliver consistency over time are the ones who help you grow. Once those relationships are broken, they're not always easy to rebuild.

Ellen learned this lesson the hard way, and her experience stands as a caution to every entrepreneur:

don't trade excellence for empty promises.

The Hidden Value of Professionalism

Across all three stories, Sam, Ellen, and Tony, a single truth stands out: many business owners underestimate the value of the professionals who protect them behind the scenes. Whether the issue was disrespect, misplaced trust, or outright disregard for legal guidance, each entrepreneur paid a heavy price for overlooking the people tasked with safeguarding their business.

Sam failed to appreciate the accountant who went far beyond her scope, handling HR, compliance, documentation, and crisis resolution. His lack of gratitude nearly cost him the backbone of his operations.

Ellen traded consistency for charisma and abandoned a proven partnership for promises that never materialized. In doing so, she lost clarity, efficiency, and the advisor who understood her company best.

Tony ignored professional warnings altogether and chose shortcuts over compliance. His refusal to listen didn't just create problems; it destroyed everything he had built.

These stories are not just cautionary, they are reminders.

Behind every thriving business is a circle of professionals working quietly, diligently, and strategically. CPAs, attorneys, bookkeepers, consultants, and compliance experts do far more than manage paperwork, they protect reputations, prevent legal disasters, and create the structure that allows businesses to scale safely.

Entrepreneurs often celebrate big wins, sales milestones, and expansion plans. But sustained success depends just as much on the people who keep the foundation steady, especially when the owner doesn't fully see the weight they carry.

Business Lessons

What These Stories Teach Every Business Owner

1. Professional advisors are not optional, they are essential.
2. They guard your business from risks you can't always see, and their expertise provides structure, stability, and protection.
3. Appreciation is a form of leadership.
4. Respecting and valuing your team builds stronger partnerships, better communication, and long-term loyalty.
5. Consistency is more valuable than charisma.
6. Trust the professional who delivers accuracy, clarity, and reliability, not the one who makes bold promises without proof.
7. Listening is a business strategy.
8. When advisors warn you about risks or compliance issues, they're protecting your livelihood, not hindering your progress.
9. Burning bridges can cost you more than you expect.
10. Once trust is broken, the professionals who once supported you may not be willing or able to return.
11. Growth requires the right people.
12. Your advisors are part of your infrastructure. Choosing them wisely and respecting their guidance is a long-term investment in your success.

Conclusion

The strongest entrepreneurs understand that success isn't built alone. It is built through partnerships with advisors who think beyond today, protect your business from tomorrow's dangers, and guide you toward long-term growth.

Respect their expertise. Value their insight. Listen to their warnings.

Because ignoring the professionals who safeguard your business doesn't just create problems, it invites consequences.

And sometimes, as these stories show, those consequences are irreversible.

Chapter 19
A Legacy Unpassed

Some business owners leave footprints that stretch far beyond the work they do. They leave a legacy not just through the business they built, but through the character they carried.

One of my longtime clients, whom I'll call Mr. H, owned and operated a successful tour bus company for more than 35 years. His business was built on consistency, relationships, and good old-fashioned hard work. It supported his family, served thousands of customers, and became known across several states for exceptional service.

But what truly made Mr. H unforgettable was him.

He treated everyone with kindness, auditors, customers, tourists, even people who arrived angry or impatient. Nothing shook his spirit. I watched him handle heated situations that would frustrate most business owners, yet he always responded with patience and grace.

One day, I asked him how he stayed so calm. He chuckled and replied, "It comes with age."

I didn't know then that it would be one of our last conversations.

We had a meeting scheduled, but he called that morning to say he wasn't feeling well. He thought it was just a cold and wanted to rest. That night, he took NyQuil.

And tragically, he never woke up.

A week later, I received a call from his number. I answered with excitement, ready to reschedule our appointment. Instead, I heard a soft, trembling voice, his daughter. She gently told me her father had passed and asked if I could help them finalize the books so the business could be sold.

I broke down in tears.

She let me cry, and when the silence settled, I asked why they were choosing to sell such a well-established business.

Her answer was heartbreaking.

She and her mother knew nothing about the operations. They had never been involved in the daily decisions, the customer relationships, the schedules, or the business systems. They felt disconnected from a company that took up so much of the man they loved.

Then she said words I'll never forget:

"We feel like the business took him from us, and we want nothing to do with it."

I helped them complete the transition and worked closely with the new owners to maintain what Mr. H had built. But for months, even years, I found myself wondering…

What if he had taught his daughter how to run the company? What if his wife had been included in the decisions? Would they have felt differently about the business? Would they have wanted to continue his legacy instead of letting it go?

This wasn't just the loss of a man, it was the loss of his life's work.

Business Lessons

What This Story Teaches Every Entrepreneur

1. A business built around one person is fragile.
2. If only one person knows the operations, relationships, and structure, the business is always at risk of collapsing without them.
3. Succession planning is not optional.
4. Document your processes, train someone else, and make sure at least one person could step in if needed.
5. Involve your family or trusted partners early.
6. When loved ones understand the business, they gain emotional buy-in and may carry the legacy forward with pride.
7. Systems protect your legacy.
8. Written procedures, passwords, vendor lists, and financial records ensure continuity, not confusion.
9. Your "why" matters.
10. Sharing the purpose behind your business helps others see the vision and value, not just the workload.
11. Time spent building relationships is as important as the revenue itself.
12. People don't inherit passion by accident, they inherit it through exposure.

Conclusion

Entrepreneurship isn't only about building income; it's about building something that can live beyond you. Mr. H created a remarkable company, but without a succession plan or shared knowledge, his family was left overwhelmed, disconnected, and unable to continue what he had started.

His legacy could have been a gift, a generational opportunity, a family asset, a continuation of his life's work.

Instead, it became something they released because they didn't know how to hold onto it.

Let this be a reminder to every business owner:

Don't wait until it's too late to bring others in.

Teach your loved ones.

Document your systems.

Share your purpose.

Build a business that can stand even when you're not there to hold it up.

Legacy isn't just about what you build,

it's about who you build it with,

and whether the people you love feel equipped to carry it forward.

Part Two

Business With No Heir

Bob was the definition of a self-made entrepreneur. For more than 25 years, he built a thriving real estate empire, buying, renovating, and managing over 30 rental properties across multiple states. He had developments underway, deals constantly moving, and a work ethic that outpaced everyone around him. Bob wasn't just involved in his business, he was the business.

He oversaw contractors, reviewed deals, approved budgets, negotiated contracts, and made every major decision himself. He wore it like a badge of honor.

But it came at a cost.

Bob pushed himself relentlessly. When he started feeling unusually tired, he chalked it up to long hours. A doctor's visit revealed dangerously high blood pressure, and he was prescribed medication to stabilize it. The side effects drained him, but Bob had no intention of slowing down.

During a weekend golf game, he mentioned feeling cold and weak, but still played the full round. By the next week, he was still unwell and reluctantly took a short break from work. True to form, he returned as soon as he could, determined not to fall behind.

Then the unthinkable happened.

While sitting at his desk giving instructions to his assistant, Bob stood up and said he needed to go home. He never made it to the door. He collapsed from a massive heart attack, gone instantly.

The shock rippled through both his family and his business.

His wife and son were devastated. The man who had been their foundation, emotionally, financially, and structurally, was suddenly gone. And the empire he spent decades building was suddenly an overwhelming burden. Neither his wife nor his son had ever been involved in the operations. They had no understanding of the contracts, the property management systems, the renovations in progress, or the financial commitments tied to each property.

For weeks, his wife couldn't even open the books. When she finally did, she realized she didn't want any part of it. To her, the business felt like the very thing that took her husband away. She wanted peace, not pressure.

With no knowledge, no training, and no guidance, the family had only one option:

sell everything.

Within months, Bob's decades of hard work, his rentals, his developments, his investments, were dismantled and sold off.

A lifetime of building disappeared in less than a year, simply because there was no plan for what would happen if he wasn't there.

Business Lessons

What Bob's Story Teaches Every Entrepreneur

1. A business built around one person is one event away from collapse.
2. No matter how successful you are, if only you know how the business runs, it cannot survive without you.
3. Emergencies don't wait for convenience.
4. Illness, injury, or incapacity can hit unexpectedly. Your family and your business must be prepared.
5. Document your processes before you need them.
6. Vendor lists, passwords, contracts, systems, financials, and workflows should be written, organized, and accessible.
7. Share the knowledge, don't carry it alone.
8. Even if your family doesn't want to run the business, they should know enough to manage, transition, or sell it properly.
9. Estate planning and succession are not only for large companies.
10. Every entrepreneur, no matter the size of the business, needs a plan for continuity.
11. Success without preparation creates unnecessary suffering.
12. Bob's family wasn't just grieving the loss of him; they were overwhelmed by the responsibility he never shared.

Conclusion

Bob built an impressive, profitable real estate empire. But without a succession plan, all that success lived and died with him. His family was left with properties they didn't understand, obligations they couldn't manage, and a business that felt more like a burden than a blessing.

The truth is simple:

Success without succession is short-lived.

A business without a plan is a business at risk.

Entrepreneurs must recognize that what they build is not only for themselves, it's for the people they love. Your family deserves clarity, education, and preparation, not confusion and overwhelming responsibility.

Because the business you build for them can only benefit them if they know how to carry it forward.

Part Three

When Tragedy Ends a Dynasty

Elizabeth was a powerhouse in the car rental industry. She had inherited her father's 40-year-old business and transformed it into something even stronger. What began as a single-location operation with 50 rental cars grew under her leadership into a multi-location enterprise with a fleet of over 100 vehicles.

Her staff trusted her, her customers respected her, and her family admired her relentless dedication. With no spouse or children, the business was her identity, her purpose, and her pride.

But everything changed in one horrifying moment.

One afternoon, a customer stormed into one of her locations furious about a 200 dollar charge. According to the rental system and the signed contract, the fees were valid, fuel charges and toll violations that were clearly itemized.

Her employees tried to calm him, but he grew more aggressive. Elizabeth overheard the commotion and, as she had done many times before, stepped in with patience and professionalism.

This time, patience couldn't save her.

In a violent outburst, the customer pulled out a gun and opened fire. Elizabeth was shot twice in the chest and died instantly. Two employees were hit, one killed, the other critically injured.

By the time law enforcement arrived, the damage was irreversible.

A life was taken. A team was shattered. A legacy was interrupted.

And the business, a thriving, respected company, was left with no one equipped to lead it.

With Elizabeth gone, the responsibility fell to her elderly parents and her only sibling, a brother who had never shown interest in the business. Instead of honoring what she built, he drained the company's resources on personal luxuries, vacations, cars, and spending sprees.

Within a year, the business that had flourished for decades was bankrupt.

Not because it wasn't profitable. Not because the market had changed.

But because no one else was prepared to carry the legacy forward.

Business Lessons

What Elizabeth's Story Teaches Every Entrepreneur

1. Tragedy can end a business overnight if no one else is prepared.
2. Even the strongest, most successful businesses collapse without a second-in-command or clear contingency plan.
3. Succession planning isn't just for retirement, it's for protection.
4. Unexpected events, violence, illness, or emergencies can strike without warning. Your business must be ready.
5. Being the only one who knows how the business runs is a dangerous risk.
6. If all the knowledge lives in your head, the business is one crisis away from dying with you.
7. Legacy requires structure, not assumptions.
8. If family or staff are never trained, informed, or included, they cannot protect what you leave behind.
9. Identifying a successor is essential.
10. Whether it's family, a trusted manager, or an outside buyer, someone must be ready to take the reins.
11. Documentation is a silent form of leadership.
12. Written procedures, operations manuals, vendor lists, passwords, and financial systems allow continuity even in crisis.
13. Love alone won't save your business, preparation will.
14. Elizabeth's family adored her, but they lacked the knowledge and roadmap needed to continue her work.

Conclusion

Elizabeth's legacy didn't end because she failed, it ended because no one else was prepared to protect it. Her decades of growth, her father's foundation, her staff's loyalty, and her own life's work disappeared simply because the business depended entirely on her.

This story delivers a sobering truth:

If your business can't survive without you, then it's not a legacy, it's a liability.

Entrepreneurs must look beyond today's success and plan for tomorrow's reality. That means:

- Training your team
- Involving your family
- Documenting processes
- Building a succession plan
- Communicating your vision

Because no matter how strong your business is, it will not matter if no one knows how to keep it alive when you're gone.

The Cost of Not Preparing for the Future

The stories of the tour bus owner, Bob the real estate investor, and Elizabeth the car rental entrepreneur share one painful thread:

They built powerful businesses,

But never built a future beyond themselves.

Each of them worked tirelessly, made sacrifices, and created opportunities. Yet when tragedy struck, through illness, sudden death, or unexpected violence, their businesses collapsed not because they were weak, but because no one else was equipped to continue them.

Their families were left grieving and overwhelmed, not only by the loss of a loved one, but by the responsibility of navigating businesses they were never included in.

Legacies that took decades to build dissolved in months.

The truth is undeniable:

Success is not measured only by what you build, but by what you prepare to leave behind.

Final Lessons for Every Business Owner

1. Success requires succession.
2. Without a plan, even the strongest business will crumble.
3. Your legacy must be shared to survive.
4. Include your family, train your leaders, and communicate your vision.
5. Prepare for emergencies, not just retirement.
6. Illness, tragedy, or sudden incapacity can strike at any time.
7. Systems create stability.
8. Documentation, manuals, financial structure, and trained personnel protect your company long after you're gone.
9. Your business is a gift, treat it like one.
10. Don't leave your family confusion; leave them clarity and direction.

Chapter 20
The Cost of a Kind Heart

Jimmy was the kind of business owner everyone loved. His shop was always busy, his customers were loyal, and his reputation in the community was spotless. But what people admired most wasn't his skill or his prices, it was his heart.

Jimmy never said no.

If a customer was short on money, he'd say, "Don't worry about it."

If a client needed time to pay, he'd say, "Pay me later."

If a family member had a hardship, Jimmy would pull out his checkbook without hesitation.

For years, it seemed harmless. His business stayed open, customers praised him, and Jimmy built a reputation as the most generous man in town.

But slowly, things started falling apart.

Despite strong revenue, Jimmy's bank account was shrinking. When tax season came, his accountant delivered tough news: almost everything Jimmy gave away wasn't tax deductible. It wasn't a business expense. It was personal giving disguised as generosity.

And it was draining him.

Then came the call that broke him.

His daughter called, stressed and in need. She asked for money, confident Jimmy would help because he always had. But this time, Jimmy didn't have it. For the first time in her life, he had to say "no."

She didn't take it well. She cried, yelled, and accused him of not caring. She hung up, and Jimmy spent the night pacing, calling, apologizing, praying she would understand.

The next morning, trying to focus on work, one of his longtime clients walked into the shop. The man said he needed help immediately but asked if he could pay the following week. Jimmy, still financially strapped, explained he needed the money upfront for parts. The client frowned, said he'd come back later…

He never did.

Jimmy later heard the customer went to a competitor instead.

That moment changed everything.

After years of giving, helping, supporting, and saying yes, Jimmy realized something painful:

When he needed others, they disappeared.

Tired, broke, and overwhelmed, he finally asked for help. He hired an accountant and a manager to dig into the numbers and restructure his business.

What they found shook him to his core.

In less than a year, Jimmy had given away over 111,000 dollars in free work, discounts, waived fees, and favors. That money could have strengthened his business, paid his bills, helped his employees, and funded his retirement, but instead, it was gone.

Jimmy wasn't just generous.

He was operating without boundaries, and it nearly cost him everything.

Business Lessons

What Jimmy's Story Teaches Every Business Owner

1. Generosity without structure becomes financial self-sabotage.
2. Being kind-hearted doesn't mean giving away your livelihood.
3. Discounts must serve a purpose, not drain your profit.
4. Every price reduction impacts your revenue, taxes, and long-term stability.
5. Emotional decisions can damage a business.
6. Helping everyone may feel good, but it must be balanced with policies and limits.
7. Clear payment terms protect both you and your customers.
8. Deposits and upfront payments are not rude, they are professional.
9. Family emergencies require personal funds, not business accounts.
10. Separating business and personal finances prevents emotional spending from sinking your company.
11. You must learn to say "no" or your business will suffer.
12. Boundaries are not cold, they are responsible and necessary.
13. The people who respect you will stay, even when you enforce rules.
14. If someone leaves because you ask for payment, they were never truly loyal.

Conclusion

Jimmy learned the hard way that a kind heart without boundaries can become a burden. His generosity was beautiful, but it lacked discipline. The moment he needed understanding or support, the same people he helped were nowhere to be found.

But with structure, accountability, and healthier habits, Jimmy rebuilt himself and his business. He didn't stop being generous, he simply became wise about his giving. His relationships improved, his stress decreased, and his finances stabilized.

Jimmy regained control, not just of his business, but of his peace.

Final Lesson:

Giving is a blessing, but only when it doesn't destroy your foundation.

Help others, but protect yourself.

Give with love, but also with limits.

Because you cannot pour from an empty cup.

Part One

When Taking Becomes Too Much

Jody was sharp, confident, and financially successful. As a respected financial planner and business strategist, she had built a thriving client base. People loved working with her. They praised her expertise, relied on her advice, and showed their appreciation in big ways, such as designer bags, expensive jewelry, concert tickets, and even luxury dinners on vacations.

Jody never asked for these gifts, but she never refused them either. She enjoyed the attention. She enjoyed being spoiled. And slowly, without realizing it, she became comfortable receiving but never giving back.

She didn't send holiday cards. She didn't say thank you with small gestures.

She didn't acknowledge birthdays or milestones.

She believed her service alone was enough.

That same pattern flowed into her personal life.

Whenever Jody called a friend, sibling, or romantic partner, the conversations always centered around her problems, never theirs. If something went wrong, she'd hint at needing help without asking directly. A bill is due. A broken appliance. A bad week. Someone would eventually offer assistance, and she welcomed it.

For years, people responded to her needs.

Until, slowly, they didn't. Family calls went unanswered. Texts were ignored.

People grew distant, but Jody didn't notice. Then came the family gathering.

Determined to confront her relatives for "acting funny," Jody showed up ready to call everyone out. But she immediately felt the shift. People were polite but distant. They talked to her briefly and quickly excused themselves.

Finally, she pulled her cousin aside and demanded to know why he hadn't been answering her calls.

His words hit harder than she expected.

"Because you're always begging, Jody. Not for money, but with your problems. The conversations always revolve around you. You don't ask about us. You don't check in. And when we help, we don't hear from you again until the next crisis. It's draining."

Jody snapped back, denying everything.

But then he said something that froze her:

"One of your clients, you know, the one who gave you those show tickets, told me he's planning to cancel. He said you only take. You don't give energy, you don't give gratitude. You just take."

Jody stormed out that day furious… but deep down, the anger wasn't at him, it was at the truth she didn't want to face.

She had alienated people. She had taken without giving.

She had relied on relationships she never invested in.

For the first time in her life, Jody had to confront that she wasn't the victim, she was the cause.

Business Lessons

What Jody's Story Teaches Every Entrepreneur

1. Relationships thrive on reciprocity, not one-sidedness.
2. Whether business or personal, people eventually pull back when they feel drained.
3. Appreciation must be expressed, not assumed.
4. A simple thank-you card, kind gesture, or recognition goes further than lavish gifts.
5. Emotional taking is still taking.
6. You don't have to ask for money to drain people; constant problems without care for others push them away.
7. Clients notice more than your services.

8. How you show gratitude affects loyalty. Clients leave when they feel unappreciated.
9. Professional success doesn't excuse personal neglect.
10. Being busy doesn't justify being self-centered. Relationships require effort.
11. Giving builds character, connection, and credibility.
12. People invest in people who invest back.
13. Self-awareness is a business skill.
14. Knowing how you show up in relationships impacts your reputation and your brand.

Conclusion

Jody learned that a life built only on receiving eventually becomes lonely. Success had blinded her to the importance of gratitude, reciprocity, and emotional presence. But once she faced the truth, she began the slow, necessary work of change.

She apologized. She rebuilt.

She started giving not just money but also time, attention, and appreciation.

Over time, the people around her opened their hearts again. Her client relationships improved. Her family reconnected. And she rediscovered what it means to be part of real, mutual relationships.

Final Takeaway:

Gratitude must be shown, not assumed.

Giving is more than money, it's presence, kindness, and sincerity.

And when you learn to give from the heart, people begin to give back, not because they have to, but because they want to.

Part Two

The Silent Cost of Silence

Prince was the quiet backbone of a successful tool rental shop that had been thriving for more than 12 years. He was methodical, reliable, and exceptionally hardworking. His staff respected him, but most customers never knew he was the owner. Prince stayed in the back, inspecting returned tools, checking inventory, and making sure transactions were accurate.

He avoided small talk. He avoided confrontation. He avoided the spotlight.

As long as the business ran smoothly, Prince believed silence was the safest approach.

Then one afternoon, everything changed.

A customer returned a rented tool expecting to receive his deposit back. But when Prince examined the equipment, several parts were broken. The tool was unusable, and the deposit needed to be withheld. Prince quietly shared this with his staff, who prepared to explain it to the customer.

The customer overheard and exploded.

"Why are you talking about me like I'm not standing right here?" he snapped. "This thing was already damaged when I got it!"

Prince didn't respond. He simply pulled the signed rental agreement and handed it to his employee to explain. The customer grew even angrier and demanded to speak to the owner.

When the staff pointed to Prince, the man scoffed.

"Him? He won't talk. He won't look at me. This is the owner?"

The customer took out his phone and began recording. He posted the video online, accusing the business of poor customer service and unprofessional leadership.

The video went viral.

The policies of the business were correct, but viewers didn't care. They criticized the lack of communication, the silence, and the awkwardness of an owner who wouldn't engage with a paying customer.

What hurt Prince the most were the comments from longtime clients:

"I never even knew he was the owner."

"He's never spoken to me, not once."

"No wonder issues aren't handled well. He hides."

For years, Prince believed staying behind the scenes kept things peaceful.

Now his silence had become the business's biggest liability.

Business Lessons

What Prince's Story Teaches Every Entrepreneur

1. Silence can be misinterpreted.
2. What feels comfortable to you may look like disrespect, avoidance, or poor customer service to others.
3. Customers want connection, not just service.

4. In today's relational, digital world, people value communication as much as the product.
5. Leaders must be visible.
6. You don't need to be outgoing, but you must show up. People follow the person they know, not the one they never see.
7. Communication protects your business.
8. A simple greeting, explanation, or acknowledgment can prevent misunderstandings and negative publicity.
9. You need the right people in the right roles.
10. If you're not comfortable being the face of the business, hire someone who is, but don't disappear completely.
11. Your online presence matters.
12. Social media can build your reputation or destroy it. Managing it proactively is essential.
13. Engagement builds trust.
14. Customers want to feel seen, heard, and valued. Silence creates distance.

Conclusion

Prince learned that being quiet isn't a problem, but disappearing is. He didn't need to become an extrovert or change who he was. He simply needed to step up as a leader, communicate more, and allow customers to connect with the person behind the business.

Once he made those changes, his reputation began to heal. Clients appreciated seeing him. Small interactions, eye contact, a greeting, a simple "thank you," transformed how people viewed the business.

The lesson:

Even the quietest leader must find a way to show up.

Leadership isn't only the work you do behind the scenes, it's the presence you bring when it matters.

Chapter 21
The Cost of Jumping Too Soon

A Costly Diversion — Linda's Story

Linda Graham had worked hard to build her financial firm from the ground up. For nearly five years, she showed up early, stayed late, and poured everything she had into building a reputation for accuracy, trust, and professionalism. By the time she hired her fourth employee, the business was stable, profitable, and finally giving her the kind of peace she had prayed for.

Her savings reflected that success. Across her accounts, she had tucked away more than 150,000 dollars, money she viewed as her family's safety net and her firm's emergency shield.

One afternoon, while reviewing documents with a long-time client in the trucking industry, she heard about an opportunity that made her pause. The client raved about the logistics company he worked with, high-paying routes, consistent work, and fast returns. Then he said the magic words every entrepreneur has heard at least once:

"If you buy a truck and partner with my company, you'll make your investment back in six months."

The idea sounded almost too good to be true. And because her husband was already a truck driver, it felt like the perfect chance to create a family-owned side business, something that could eventually produce passive income for them all.

Excited, Linda shared the idea with her husband. He lit up. Their son agreed it was smart. The family jumped into action, visiting dealerships and researching trucks. Eventually, they found one at Kenworth. It was 90,000 dollars with a $36,000 down payment.

To Linda, it seemed like a calculated risk. She trusted her client, trusted her husband's industry experience, and trusted her ability to manage money.

But trust without due diligence is expensive.

After only a few loads, the truck broke down. The dealership covered the first set of repairs under pressure, but the pattern didn't stop. Within the first three months, they spent over 20,000 dollars on repairs. Over the next year, breakdown after breakdown added up to nearly 90,000 dollars in repair costs alone.

Every time the truck was down, it produced zero revenue. Zero income, but the expenses never stopped, including insurance, payments, fuel costs, registration, permits, and the ongoing repairs. Linda started dipping into her savings to stay afloat. Then she started using business funds to catch up.

Little by little, her trucking investment began starving the business that had taken her years to build.

Her office rent fell behind. Payroll became a stress point. Her cushion disappeared. And one morning, a five-day notice was taped to her office door.

The golden opportunity had turned into a financial avalanche.

The Turning Point Refocusing on the Core

In the middle of stress, shame, and panic, Linda did something many business owners never slow down long enough to do, she sat with her mistakes and analyzed them.

She wrote down every decision she made:

- Jumping into a totally different industry without research
- Believing someone else's success story without verifying the numbers
- Using business funds to support a failing venture
- Assuming her income could carry both companies
- Neglecting the firm that fed her family

Seeing those truths in black and white was painful, but it gave her clarity.

Her first step was survival. She negotiated with her landlord and agreed to pay 1,000 dollars a week until the rent was caught up. Because she had a strong history, the landlord said yes.

Then she did the work. Linda extended her hours. She reached out to every client she had ever served. She marketed, followed up, rebuilt, and re-earned trust.

She also made the hardest decision of all, she let the trucking business go. She accepted the loss. Her husband supported the decision, acknowledging how deeply the venture had drained their savings, energy, and peace of mind.

This time, she chose her foundation.

Lessons for Business Owners

1. Don't Fund Your Dreams With Your Lifeline
2. Your main business is the engine that pays your bills, feeds your family, and secures your future.
3. A new venture should never threaten the stability of the one that keeps you standing.
4. You Cannot Skip Due Diligence

5. If someone promises fast money, high returns, or guaranteed income, your next step should be research, not a down payment.
6. Verify everything.
7. Inspect everything.
8. Run the numbers yourself.
9. Stay in Your Lane Until You're Ready to Merge
10. Just because you understand business doesn't mean you understand every business.
11. Industry knowledge matters.
12. Operational experience matters.
13. Margins, downtime, risk, and compliance all matter.
14. Emotion Makes Expensive Decisions
15. Linda wanted to support her husband. That desire was genuine, but emotional decisions often bypass the critical thinking required for safe investing.
16. When Trouble Hits, Protect Your Core First
17. You fix the business that feeds your family before you try to create one that feeds your pride.
18. Recovery Requires Humility and Hustle
19. Linda didn't blame anyone else.
20. She didn't hide.
21. She didn't run.
22. She owned the decisions and dug herself out with discipline, strategy, and consistency.

Conclusion

Digging Herself Out First

By the end of her first recovery year, Linda had caught up on rent and saved 10,000 dollars. By the next year, she added another 10,000 dollars. Slowly but surely, she rebuilt the foundation she nearly destroyed.

And with rebuilding came wisdom.

Linda learned a timeless truth:

You can't rescue anybody else if you haven't secured yourself first.

In trying to create a trucking business for her husband, she jeopardized the firm that supported the entire family. But once she refocused, she rebuilt from a place of strength, not desperation.

Today, Linda evaluates every new idea with a sharper lens:

- Does it threaten the stability of my main business
- Is this a want or a strategic move
- Have I verified the numbers myself
- Does this opportunity match my expertise, or am I chasing someone else's dream

She now leads with discipline, strategy, and experience, not excitement and assumptions.

Linda's comeback became a reminder to every business owner:

When you're in a hole, your first job is to climb out. Only then can you pull somebody else up.

Part 2

Betrayed by Her Own Vision

Ala's Story

Ala grew up in a small foreign village where culture, tradition, and family pride shaped every part of life. From a young age, she was drawn to the skill the women in her community practiced, an art form so respected and so valued that women would save for months just to receive it. Ala wasn't just good at it; she had a gift.

By the time she was 12, she was already teaching others, carrying the legacy of generations before her.

When her family moved to the United States, Ala carried that gift with her. Her parents opened several small businesses, and Ala, now a teenager in a new country, worked tirelessly for them. She never asked for a paycheck. She simply believed that family came first. Her work contributed to their success, and once her parents became self-sufficient, they released her from her promise.

Adulthood came quickly, and with it, a marriage to a man much older than her, one her parents warned her against. But like many young women searching for independence, Ala believed love, loyalty, and hard work could overcome anything.

Her husband encouraged her to open a business using the cultural skill she mastered as a child. Ala trusted him. She formed a small team with a few friends, and together they built something beautiful. Her services were in high demand. Her practice grew so rapidly that she opened a second location and began training other young women, just as she had done back home.

But behind the scenes, something else was happening.

Ala worked long hours. She cared for two children. She perfected her craft. Her clients adored her.

Meanwhile, her husband handled the business side, or so he said. He never touched the technical work. He didn't build client relationships. He didn't understand the craft. But he was the one managing the money.

Ala didn't question it. She believed that if her husband was providing for the family and the bills were paid, everything was fine.

Until the marriage collapsed.

After 15 years of emotional strain, Ala finally gathered the strength to leave. But what followed was a storm she never saw coming. Her husband demanded half of everything, business included. He even trained his sister in Ala's technique, anticipating taking over what Ala had built with her hands, mind, and heart.

Suspicious and heartbroken, Ala hired an accountant to review their financial history.

The truth nearly broke her.

- He had taken almost every dollar the business made.
- He filed for two rounds of PPP loans without telling her.
- He secured an SBA loan in the business's name, completely behind her back.
- The money was gone.
- All financial records were controlled by him.

Ala had nothing but shock and a long legal battle ahead.

Her house was sold. Her savings drained. Emotional stress pushed her away from clients. Her thriving business, once her pride, crumbled under the weight of betrayal and financial abuse.

Yet even after losing so much, Ala refused to lose herself.

Taking Back Her Power

The Rebuild

Broken but not defeated, Ala made a decision:

She was going to rebuild her life and her business, and this time, no one would ever control her again.

With almost no money, she restarted small, one client at a time. She rented tiny spaces, offered her services independently, and slowly rebuilt her reputation. But this time, she did something she had never done before:

She took full control. She set up new systems. Opened new business accounts.

Tracked every dollar. Learned financial literacy. Learned legal compliance.

Learned how to protect herself.

Then she did something even more powerful, she turned her pain into purpose.

Ala began teaching immigrant women how to start and manage their own businesses. She created programs that helped them:

- Understand the legal side of business ownership
- Track income properly
- Apply for grants and loans with transparency
- Structure their businesses to protect themselves
- Separate personal finances from business finances
- Create safeguards in marriage and partnerships

She spoke openly about her own mistakes, not to shame herself, but to protect the next woman who didn't know what she didn't know.

And her students listened. Because Ala wasn't just teaching from theory; she was teaching from scars.

Through her mentorship, dozens of women launched stable, legal, well-structured businesses, changing the economic future of their families.

Lessons for Business Owners

1. Talent Is Not Enough, You Must Understand Your Money
2. Ala had a rare skill, a loyal clientele, and a booming business, but zero understanding of her financial picture.
3. Your talent can grow the business.
4. But only financial literacy can protect it.
5. Never Hand Over Full Control to Anyone
6. Not your partner.
7. Not your spouse.
8. Not your family.
9. Collaboration is healthy.
10. Blind trust is dangerous.
11. Business requires oversight, documentation, and accountability, even with people you love.
12. If Your Name Is on the Business, Your Eyes Must Be on the Books
13. You don't have to be an accountant, but you must:
    - Know where your money is
    - See your bank statements
    - Understand your financial obligations
    - Monitor loans, grants, and liabilities

1. Your business should never surprise you.
2. Love Doesn't Replace Legal Protection
3. Marriage does not cancel the need for boundaries.
4. Romance does not replace responsibility.
5. And trust does not negate oversight.
6. Every business owner needs:
    - Operating agreements
    - Access to accounts
    - Proof of income
    - Clear financial responsibilities

1. Protection is not disrespect.
2. Protection is wisdom.
3. Pain Can Become Purpose
4. Ala's business was stolen from her twice.
5. But her comeback allowed hundreds of women to avoid the same fate.
6. Sometimes your greatest hurt becomes your greatest assignment.

Conclusion

Ala's story is not a tragedy.

It is a rebirth.

She lost her home, her savings, her stability, and the business she built with her own hands. But she gained freedom, clarity, and a deeper purpose. Today, she runs a thriving business once again, but this time, she runs it with knowledge, structure, and complete ownership.

She no longer views her past as something to hide. She sees it as the foundation of her calling.

Ala now teaches women how to:

- Own their businesses fully
- Protect themselves financially
- Build systems that safeguard their future
- Advocate for themselves with confidence

Through loss, she found her legacy. Her message to every woman, and every business owner, is clear:

Do not give away your power. Not in love. Not in business. Not ever.

Part 3

The Rise and Betrayal

Virginia's Story

Virginia was the kind of woman people noticed, beautiful, creative, warm, and full of ambition. She had the vision and work ethic of a natural entrepreneur. When she met her future husband, a charismatic physical trainer, she believed she had found the perfect partner in business and in life. Together, they dreamed of building a brand centered on health, wellness, and financial independence.

Shortly after marrying, they moved to a new state to launch a healthy food company, meals and protein snacks designed for athletes, gym-goers, and busy families. Virginia was the engine behind the operation:

- She created the recipes.
- She managed production.
- She negotiated store contracts.
- She set up operations and systems.

Her husband brought enthusiasm and image, but Virginia was the one executing the vision.

Their hard work paid off. Virginia negotiated with multiple 7-Eleven stores to carry their branded freezer units, a huge milestone for any small business. She secured partnerships, streamlined the business, and built trust in their community.

Then came their biggest victory:

School district contracts to provide healthy meals for students. It was the kind of deal that could change a family's trajectory. Virginia felt proud, accomplished, and aligned with her purpose.

For two and a half years, they appeared to be a rising power couple, thriving in life and business.

But behind the scenes, everything was shifting. And Virginia didn't see the signs until it was too late.

Her husband began quietly removing her from the very business she helped build:

• First, he took over school kitchen operations.

• Then he managed payroll.

• Then he locked her out of the business bank accounts.

• Finally, he removed her name entirely from the LLC documents.

When she confronted him, hoping for clarity, he delivered the final blow:

"This business was always mine. I'm taking it in a different direction."

The betrayal was devastating.

The man she trusted had quietly pushed her out of her own creation. His attitude became harsher, the verbal abuse escalated, and within weeks he asked for a divorce. Virginia spiraled into depression. She had uprooted her life, moved her family, built a dream, and ended up with nothing, not even the business she had poured her soul into.

But even in her darkest moment, something within her refused to stay down.

Building From the Ground Up

For Herself

Heartbroken but determined, Virginia hired an attorney to uncover what had happened behind the scenes. The findings only confirmed the manipulation she already suspected. But instead of drowning in anger, she decided to use it as fuel.

She did something brave:

She went back to the very vendors, partners, and stores she once brought into the business, alone.

Virginia told the truth. She explained her situation with honesty, humility, and professionalism. And because she had always been the backbone of the operation, every vendor remembered her work ethic. They didn't hesitate to support her comeback.

This time, Virginia built her vision her way.

She shifted from full meals to portable, protein-packed healthy treats, easy for athletes, commuters, parents, and students. These treats could be eaten anytime, before workouts, during long work hours, or late at night without guilt. Practical. Nutritious. Scalable.

She rented a commercial kitchen. She started fresh production.

And then she did something bold and fearless:

She expanded back to her home state and opened a second location.

Within months, Virginia was operating in two states, independently, confidently, and successfully.

When her ex-husband learned about her comeback, he reached out, full of apologies, regret, and soft words. But Virginia had learned long ago that not every apology is sincere.

She shut the door. For good.

Lessons for Business Owners

1. Contribution Isn't Ownership Without Documentation
2. Virginia built the business, but her name wasn't protected.
3. If you're contributing your skills, labor, or ideas, your paperwork must match your reality.
4. Never Ignore Financial Access and Control
5. Healthy relationships do not require secret passwords or hidden accounts.
6. If you can't see the money, you're not part of the business, you're labor.
7. Business Structure Must Match the Partnership You Believe You Have
8. Verbal promises mean nothing in court.
9. Operating agreements, EIN ownership, and bank access determine who truly holds power.
10. Loyalty Should Never Replace Legal Protection
11. You can love someone deeply and still protect your assets.
12. Contracts are not a lack of trust, they are a protection of clarity.
13. Relationships Built on Purpose Should Not Erase Your Identity
14. Virginia made the business her identity, and when it was taken, she felt empty.
15. Your business is a part of you, not the whole of you.
16. Betrayal Can Be the Beginning of Reinvention
17. She was left with nothing, but her talent, resilience, and relationships helped her rebuild stronger than before.

Conclusion

Empowered Through Experience

Virginia's journey is a powerful reminder that success built through someone else's approval is fragile, but success built through your own ownership is unshakeable.

She learned the hard way that:

- Business ownership must be protected.
- Marriage does not replace accountability.
- Love cannot cancel legal rights.
- Your contributions matter, but only if they are documented.

Today, Virginia operates with clarity, confidence, and total independence. She no longer builds someone else's dream at the cost of her own. She builds for herself, protects herself, and thrives because of herself.

Her story stands as a message to every woman in business:

Never hand over your power, not for love, not for partnership, and not for the illusion of security.

Virginia didn't just survive betrayal. She turned it into her greatest comeback.

Chapter 22
The Unattended Business

The Story — When Success Isn't Supervised

Dave was known across town as the young man who turned a simple repair shop into a local success story. He had community support, a talented team, and steady business coming through the doors. On the outside, everything looked flawless. Customers trusted him. Employees respected him. The shop was always busy.

But behind the scenes, a different picture was unfolding.

As the business grew, Dave slowly stepped back, not intentionally, but gradually. He became less involved in the day-to-day operations and relied heavily on his employees to keep things running smoothly. The problem wasn't delegation; it was disconnection. Dave wasn't present. He wasn't organized. And he wasn't leading.

Last-minute deliveries became routine. Employees would get only 20 or 30 minutes' notice before a school or client pickup. They were frustrated, stressed, and embarrassed. They were covering for Dave more than they were following him.

One morning, everything changed.

Dave asked one of his most loyal and dependable employees to handle another last-minute school delivery. The employee stood his ground, something he had never done.

"I'm not doing it today. I've told you before, stop giving me these last-minute orders. It makes me look unprofessional. I won't let you damage my reputation."

Dave had no choice but to deliver the order himself.

When he arrived at the school, he was greeted by a student with an honesty most adults avoid:

"Why are you guys always late? We only have 45 minutes in this class, and we always have to rearrange everything because of you. Everyone else comes on time except your company."

Dave apologized, embarrassed.

The student replied:

"You said that last time. But you were still late."

That moment hit Dave harder than any business setback ever had.

On the drive back, he sat in his car replaying the words. He knew the child was right. He had allowed bad habits to turn into business standards, and the people around him were feeling the consequences.

When Dave returned to the shop, he pulled aside the employee who refused the delivery. This time, the employee didn't hold back.

"Dave, your business is great, but you're not in it anymore. We're carrying the load while you're in and out, on your phone, or running errands. Some client orders sit for months. This business will fall apart if you don't change. And if something doesn't shift soon, I'm leaving."

It was the wake-up call Dave needed.

He realized the business wasn't failing because of a lack of talent, customers, or opportunity. It was failing because he wasn't leading it.

The habits he had abandoned his business to develop had taken years to build, and they wouldn't disappear overnight. But he knew one thing: if he didn't fix himself, he would lose everything he'd built.

The Solution

Rebuilding From the Inside Out

Dave didn't make excuses. He didn't blame the team. He didn't minimize the problem. He took responsibility and committed to becoming the leader his business needed.

He implemented strategic changes that transformed the shop:

1. **Scheduled Deliveries and Operations**

Dave created a clear, consistent operating schedule:

- All deliveries are assigned at least 24 hours in advance
- No more last-minute scrambling
- No surprises for employees or customers
- Structure replaced chaos.

2. **Accountability Meetings**

He hired a part-time operations consultant to review:

3. • Repair timelines

- Customer follow-ups

- Employee tasks
- System updates

Weekly accountability kept the business moving forward.

4. **Presence and Time Boundaries**

Dave committed to six uninterrupted hours in the shop daily:

- No social calls
- No personal errands
- No disappearing acts

His presence shifted the culture instantly.

5. **Customer Order Tracking System**

A large tracking board was installed so everyone could see:

- What repairs were in progress
- What was delayed
- Who was assigned to what
- When customers could expect completion

Transparency created professionalism.

6. **Empowering the Team**

Dave sat down with each employee and asked for honest feedback. Their words became the foundation of new policies.

He gave them more decision-making authority within their roles, something that instantly boosted confidence and morale.

7. **Rebuilding the Brand's Reputation**

Dave personally contacted every client with overdue repairs:

- He apologized
- He offered priority service
- He gave accurate timelines
- He committed to improvement

He even returned to the school to speak with the teacher and students, assuring them that the company's standards had changed.

This time, he backed his apology with action.

Lessons for Business Owners

1. **A Business Can't Run Itself**

Delegation is powerful, but disconnection is destructive.

Your team can support the business, but they cannot replace your leadership.

2. **Last-Minute Habits Damage Professionalism**

Rushed work becomes poor work.

Surprises lead to stress.

Disorganization destroys trust.

3. **Your Team Mirrors Your Habits**

If you're inconsistent, they'll be inconsistent.

If you're absent, they'll disconnect.

If you don't care about the schedule, they won't either.

Leadership isn't what you say, it's what you model.

4. **Accountability Is a Tool, Not a Punishment**

Bringing in outside oversight helped Dave refocus.

Every business needs structure, check-ins, and follow-through.

5. **Presence Builds Culture**

Business owners sometimes forget that their physical presence communicates:

- Commitment
- Standards
- Expectations
- Professionalism

You can't lead from the parking lot.

6. **Reputation Is Built Daily**

One late delivery won't ruin a business, but a pattern will.

Customers don't measure you by your intentions, they measure you by their experience.

Conclusion

Showing Up Is the Real Leadership

Dave's story proves a timeless truth:

Starting a business is easy.

Showing up for it every day is the real work.

His absence didn't destroy his business overnight. It happened slowly, silently, one missed deadline and one distracted day at a time. It took the honesty of an employee and the bold truth from a child to wake him up.

Today, Dave leads his business differently:

- He's present.
- He's consistent.
- He's accountable.
- He's intentional.

His name carries weight again, not because he built the shop, but because he leads it.

Every business owner must remember:

You can't grow a business you're not in.

You can't lead a team you don't guide.

And you can't create excellence if you don't show up consistently.

Dave didn't just fix his business. He fixed his leadership, and that saved everything.

Part 2

The Cost of Disrespecting Time

Cynthia had spent seven years building a name for herself in the beauty industry. Her work was unmatched, flawless installations, precise cuts, silky press-outs, and transformations that kept clients coming back. People loved her talent. But talent wasn't her problem.

Her professionalism was.

Behind the scenes, Cynthia had developed habits that chipped away at the client experience. She was consistently late, so late that it became part of her brand. Clients would pay deposits, arrive on time, then sit outside in their cars for 30 minutes to an hour, waiting for Cynthia to show up.

And when she finally arrived, she didn't start immediately. She would sit in her chair scrolling on her phone, finishing personal calls, laughing at videos, or taking breaks before even shampooing her client. A 90-minute appointment routinely stretched into four hours.

Her clients tolerated it because they loved the finished result, but frustration was building.

Then came Tina.

Tina wasn't just any client. She had influence, connections, and a respected presence in the community. She booked an appointment, paid her deposit, and made one simple request:

"I have a flight. Please, please be on time."

Cynthia promised she would.

When Tina arrived, Cynthia was indeed at the salon, but another client was still in her chair.

"Give me 10 minutes," she said casually.

Twenty minutes passed.

"Cynthia, I really need to be done by the time we discussed," Tina reminded her.

"I got you," Cynthia replied, but she didn't move any faster.

Another fifteen minutes went by, and the previous client was still in the chair.

Frustrated, Tina asked for a refund.

Cynthia refused, reminding her of the no-refund policy she enforced on everyone else, even when she was the one late.

The disagreement escalated, and Tina left. And Cynthia brushed it off, believing that losing one client wasn't a big deal.

But Tina's voice carried weight.

Within days, Cynthia saw her schedule decline. Bookings dried up. People canceled. Discount deals that once sold out in minutes sat untouched. Her phone wasn't ringing, and her chair sat empty.

The community didn't quietly slip away; they walked out loudly.

One afternoon, a long-time client returned using a half-off coupon. As Cynthia worked on her hair, the client delivered the truth Cynthia had been avoiding.

"You messed up with Tina. She could've built your business or shut it down, and you chose the wrong one."

Cynthia tried to defend herself, explaining the situation, the overlap, the delays.

The client paused and said:

"That's your problem. Not ours. We pay for professionalism, not just hair. You're always late, always on your phone, always taking breaks. It's draining. We don't feel respected."

Cynthia felt her stomach drop.

Talent had carried her, but her habits were dragging her down.

She tried reaching out to Tina, hoping for a chance to make things right, but every call went unanswered.

The silence spoke for itself.

Cynthia was left alone with the truth:

Her lack of discipline had cost her community, credibility, and cash flow.

The Solution

Rebuilding Her Standards

Cynthia realized her downfall wasn't competition or lack of talent; it was her behavior. She had disrespected the most valuable currency in service-based industries: client time.

She made the tough but necessary decision to change her entire approach. Here's what she implemented:

1. **Strict Scheduling With Buffer Times**

She upgraded her booking system to include:

- Automatic reminders
- Enforced buffer times
- No double-booking
- On-time start and finish expectations

Structure replaced chaos.

2. **Fair Deposit and Accountability Policy**

She updated her deposit terms to include:

- Partial refunds
- Service credits
- Discounts
- Apologies when she was the one late

Clients began to trust her again.

3. **A Phone-Free Service Rule**

To eliminate distractions, Cynthia set her phone to Do Not Disturb during appointments, allowing only emergency calls through the main salon line.

Her attention returned to her clients, not her notifications.

4. **Client Feedback Invitation**

Cynthia sent an apology letter to past clients, acknowledging her mistakes and asking for suggestions.

This humility opened the door for reconnection.

5. **A Professional Environment Commitment**

She implemented rules for herself:

- No loud music
- No personal conversations during services
- No unnecessary breaks
- No multitasking during a client's appointment

The salon felt peaceful again.

6. **A Business Coach for Accountability**

She hired a coach to guide her in:

- Time management
- Customer service
- Brand image
- Professional standards

Her habits shifted, and her confidence grew.

Lessons for Business Owners

1. **Customers Pay for More Than a Service**

They pay for:

- Respect
- Time
- Peace
- Professionalism

Talent attracts clients. Professionalism keeps them.

2. **Time Is a Business Owner's Biggest Liability**

   When you waste people's time, you waste their trust.

   And trust is what pays the bills.

3. **Word of Mouth Can Build You or Break You**

   A good reputation brings clients.

   A single bad experience with the right person can destroy momentum instantly.

4. **You Can't Hide Bad Habits Behind Good Work**

   Skill does not excuse unprofessional behavior.

   Clients notice everything, and they remember everything.

5. **Change Requires Ownership**

   Cynthia couldn't recover until she admitted her role in her decline.

   Every comeback starts with accountability.

Conclusion

Respect Keeps the Doors Open

Cynthia learned a hard but necessary truth:

In business, your skill may bring people to the door, but your respect keeps them from walking out.

She had the gift. She had the talent. She had the clientele. What she lacked was discipline, professionalism, and respect for the people who supported her success.

Losing Tina was painful, but it was the turning point she needed. By rebuilding her professionalism, Cynthia didn't just revive her brand, she revived her identity as a true business owner.

Because in this industry, talent opens the door…but respect, reliability, and professionalism keep it open.

Part 3

The Price of Negligence

When Carelessness Becomes Catastrophic

Jim had always dreamed of owning a small, cozy neighborhood restaurant. With just four employees and a simple menu, he created a place where people came for comfort food, good conversation, and the best fried fish in town. His fish and fries combo became a local favorite, crispy, golden, seasoned to perfection.

Jim was hands-on. He cooked most of the meals, greeted customers, and took pride in delivering food made with care. He wasn't a big franchise or a fancy restaurant, he was the heart of the community, and people loved him for it.

But one thing Jim took for granted was the seriousness of food allergies.

That oversight nearly cost someone their life, and ultimately cost him his business.

One evening, a couple walked in and ordered the fish and fries. The wife told the cashier she was allergic to a particular seasoning and needed her meal prepared without it. The cashier wrote the request clearly on the order ticket, big, bold, and underlined.

In the kitchen, the chef read the note, then ignored it.

He was overwhelmed and behind on tickets. Instead of slowing down or asking for help, he decided the request was not that serious. He added the seasoning anyway.

When the food reached the table, the couple began eating. Within minutes, the wife started gasping for air. Her throat tightened. She couldn't breathe.

Her husband panicked, asking if the seasoning was removed.

The cashier rushed to the back.

"Did you take the seasoning off?" she asked.

The chef shrugged.

"I didn't think it mattered."

Chaos broke out. The woman was going into anaphylactic shock. Her husband used her EpiPen while other customers called 911. Paramedics rushed her to the hospital.

Later that night, the furious husband returned demanding answers. When the chef admitted what he had done, the argument escalated and police were called to calm the situation.

But the damage was already done.

A lawsuit followed. The judge ruled the restaurant negligent. The financial penalties and public backlash were crushing. Jim couldn't recover. The restaurant, the place he poured his heart into, was forced to close.

Jim later admitted that the hardest part wasn't losing the business, it was knowing that someone nearly died because an employee didn't respect the seriousness of their job.

One careless decision shattered years of hard work.

The Solution

Ensuring Safety, Structure, and Standards

Jim's experience is a painful reminder that in business, negligence has consequences. Lives are impacted. Reputations collapse. And sometimes, the damage is irreversible.

Here's what could have prevented the tragedy, and what every business owner must implement:

1. **Mandatory Allergen Training**

   Every employee should be trained and certified in allergen safety. Allergies are not preferences, they are medical emergencies waiting to happen if mishandled.

2. **Clear Allergy Protocols**

   A system must exist for allergy orders, such as:

   - Verbal confirmation
   - Highlighted order tickets
   - Separate preparation areas
   - Dedicated tools to avoid cross-contamination

Food safety must never be optional.

3. **Zero-Tolerance Policy**

   Ignoring allergy instructions should result in immediate disciplinary action or termination.

   No exceptions. No excuses.

4. **Emergency Preparedness**

   Although the customer had an EpiPen, staff should be trained to:

   - Recognize allergic reactions
   - Call 911 immediately
   - Assist appropriately

   A prepared team saves lives.

5. **Hiring for Responsibility, Not Just Skill**

   Jim realized too late that technical skill in the kitchen isn't enough. Employees must share the owner's values: integrity, responsibility, and respect for customer safety.

Combined Conclusion

When Leadership Fails to Lead

Chapter 22 highlights three different stories, Dave, Cynthia, and Jim, but all point to the same underlying issue:

Negligence in leadership always becomes the downfall of a business.

Let's look at the pattern:

• **Dave**

He built a respected repair company but neglected the very structure that kept it alive. His chronic absence and poor time management created chaos. His team felt abandoned, and his customers felt ignored. Dave didn't lose business because of poor service, he lost it because he wasn't present.

• **Cynthia**

She was one of the best stylists in her city, but her reputation crumbled because she disrespected her clients' time. Her lateness, distractions, and lack of professionalism made customers feel undervalued. One influential client walked away, and the entire community followed.

• **Jim**

His food, service, and customer loyalty were undeniable. But he failed to enforce safety protocols in his kitchen. A single employee's careless decision led to a medical emergency, a lawsuit, and ultimately the closure of his restaurant.

Final Lesson

The Cost of Leadership Neglect

The downfall in each story wasn't caused by:

- A bad product
- A lack of demand
- Competition
- Poor marketing

The downfall stemmed from behavioral, habit, and leadership gaps.

These stories show one undeniable truth:

Success isn't built on talent alone. It's built on consistency, standards, and responsibility.

You can have:

- The best food
- The best service
- The best skill
- The best team

But if you fail to lead, to enforce structure, or to respect the people you serve, your business will fall behind you.

Leadership isn't about being in charge.

Leadership is about taking care of the people depending on you, employees, and customers.

The moment you stop respecting:

- Their time
- Their safety
- Their experience
- Their trust

is the moment you start losing the business you worked so hard to build.

Talent will open the door. Professionalism, discipline, and leadership will keep it open.

Chapter 23
Fast Money, Long Consequences

The Story — When the Spotlight Starts to Dim

Tam was vibrant, full of life, confidence, and style. From a young age, she loved fashion, attention, and the thrill of looking good. She craved the spotlight, and when she turned 18, she entered the exotic dancing industry. The cash flowed instantly.

And not just small amounts, real money.

She earned $12,000 to $13,000 a week, sometimes more. The lifestyle followed naturally:

- Luxury home
- High-end car
- Designer purses
- Newest phones and gadgets
- Shopping as therapy
- Vacations on impulse

She mastered charm. With her beauty, energy, and personality, she attracted generous admirers who showered her with gifts, cash, and opportunities. Life moved fast, and Tam loved every moment of it.

She raised her children with the same abundance. No expense was too big, no request too much.

But Tam never planned for tomorrow.

She didn't save. She didn't invest. She didn't think about retirement. She didn't track her cash.

Everything she earned was spent as quickly as it came in.

By her mid-30s, the world around her had changed. The industry became more regulated, more competitive, and riskier. Laws shifted. Clubs operated differently. Social media has altered how dancers earn and market themselves.

The money slowed. But the bills did not.

Her lifestyle, once easily supported by nightly income, was now a heavy burden. She had caught legal cases before, but now they felt heavier, more damaging, more permanent. Her daughter left for college, and Tam found herself asking a question she had avoided for years:

"What else can I do that pays like this?"

With no resume, no work history, and no documented income, the world outside the club felt intimidating and inaccessible.

Tam's story is not rare.

It's shared by countless women who chose industries where income is fast but financial literacy is low. Not because they're irresponsible, but because no one ever taught them how to turn fast cash into long-term stability.

And it's not just dancers.

It's barbers. Beauticians. Nail techs. Influencers. Bottle girls. Promo models. Content creators.

Anyone who earns daily or weekly cash with no structured system behind it.

Today's culture glorifies fast money but ignores the long-term consequences of not planning for a future beyond the spotlight.

The Solution

Turning Fast Money Into Forever Money

Whether you're dancing, bartending, creating content, doing hair, or anything else that brings in quick cash, the rules for long-term success are the same.

Here's how to protect yourself so you never feel trapped by the income you once enjoyed.

1. **Establish a Legal Business Entity**

Create an LLC or corporation and run all your earnings through it.

This allows you to:

- Build business credit
- Separate personal and business finances
- Apply for loans
- Protect your personal assets
- Keep accurate records

When your money has structure, opportunities open.

2. **Put Yourself on Payroll**

This strategy might be the most important one.

If you make $12,000 a week, pay yourself:

$4,000 to $5,000 as a salary.

Running payroll helps you:

- Pay into Social Security
- Build a tax record
- Qualify for mortgages and home loans
- Document your income for car financing
- Create retirement benefits
- Show financial stability

When you want to transition into a traditional industry, proof of income matters.

3. **Use Insurance Tools for Long-Term Wealth**

Invest in tools like:

- Indexed Universal Life Insurance (IULs)
- Retirement annuities
- Tax-deferred investment accounts

With discipline, these can grow into six-figure annual payouts later in life, money that continues long after your dancing or cash-based career ends.

4. **Hire a CPA and Financial Advisor but Stay Involved**

Professionals can guide you, but you must stay aware.

Read your statements. Ask questions. Understand your tax obligations. Make informed decisions.

Never allow anyone, even an expert, to control your finances without your full participation.

5. Budget and Save Consistently

You don't have to save thousands at a time. You just have to save consistently.

Allocate:

- A percentage for taxes
- A percentage for savings
- A percentage for investments
- A percentage for business expenses

Even small amounts grow when done consistently.

6. Build Self-Worth Beyond the Job

This is the emotional part.

Industries like dancing, content creation, and influencing can take a toll on self-esteem. People judge. People talk. People assume.

Build confidence that isn't tied to:

- Your looks
- The attention you receive
- Your income
- Your stage name
- Your online persona

When you believe in your value beyond your job, you make better financial decisions for your future.

Conclusion

Fast Money Requires Even Faster Planning

Tam's journey reminds us of a truth many people ignore:

Fast money feels good until it stops. Then the consequences begin.

This chapter is not about shaming women or anyone for choosing a high-earning, nontraditional path.

It's about preparing for the day the income slows, the laws change, the body ages, the industry shifts, or the opportunity fades.

Because it will fade.

Every entrepreneur, whether they dance, braid, cut hair, or create content, faces the same danger:

Earning without a plan.

When you have no plan, you wake up one day realizing the lifestyle you built is too expensive to keep.

But when you prepare early, you create:

- Options
- Safety
- Flexibility
- Dignity
- Wealth
- Freedom

Tam's story doesn't end in regret, it ends in awareness. She realized she could pivot, learn, restructure, and rebuild her future with intention.

And so can you.

Your income today does not define your outcome tomorrow.

Fast money can build real wealth if you manage it with discipline, structure, and vision.

Prepare now, so your future self can thank you later.

Part Two

The Discipline Behind the Hustle

Entrepreneurs, no matter the industry, often start their journey with big dreams, excitement, and hustle. But what many don't start with is discipline. Financial discipline, especially.

People hear the classic advice: "Save 10 percent of everything you earn."

However, when you're juggling rent, staff, inventory, taxes, kids, and personal responsibilities, 10 percent can feel impossible.

But the lesson is simple:

Start somewhere. Start small. Start now.

I remember the moment financial discipline first clicked for me. I downloaded the Acorns app and decided to try something different. I wasn't saving hundreds. I wasn't saving thousands. I started with:

- $25 into retirement
- $25 into a stock account
- $50 into a basic savings account

One hundred dollars a month.

Nothing special. Nothing glamorous. Just intentional.

I barely paid attention to it because the numbers felt too small to matter until they added up.

At the end of the year, I logged into my accounts and saw over $3,000 saved.

That moment changed my perspective. It changed my habits. It changed my financial future.

Because when you go from saving nothing to saving something, that something becomes everything.

From that point forward, I increased my contributions, explored new savings methods, and made financial protection a priority. It wasn't just about building a cushion, it was about building peace of mind.

My mother always said, "Have three months of bills saved."

But the way this economy looks today?

Three months isn't enough. Six months isn't enough.

Entrepreneurs need at least one full year of living expenses saved.

When you have a year's worth of breathing room, you make clearer decisions, take better risks, and protect your business when life throws a punch.

Because here's the truth:

When you're in survival mode, desperation makes decisions for you.

And desperation has never led an entrepreneur to success.

This is especially true for self-employed and cash-based professionals, stylists, barbers, dancers, influencers, braiders, nail techs, gig workers, and small business owners. Many hustle so hard that they forget to build safety nets that protect their future.

I've seen the consequences firsthand.

One of my clients, a hairstylist who worked independently for thirty years, reached retirement age and learned she would receive less than $900 a month in Social Security. That number broke her heart. But what broke mine was realizing she had no idea how her choices had affected her benefits.

She wasn't irresponsible. She wasn't reckless. She simply didn't know.

Too many entrepreneurs are never taught how money truly works.

Why This Conversation Matters

Entrepreneurs are more than business owners, we are providers, creators, and problem-solvers. But in the process of building everyone else's life, we often forget to build our own.

I've had countless business owners sit in my office with tears in their eyes, not because they failed, but because they finally realized no one ever told them to save, plan, invest, or prepare.

And that must change.

We must normalize:

- Wealth conversations
- Retirement planning
- Savings goals
- Financial literacy
- Accountability
- Long-term protection

These aren't luxuries, they are survival tools.

I am not sharing this from a pedestal.

I'm sharing it from experience, from mistakes, from wake-up calls, and from late financial lessons that I had to learn the hard way.

If I can fix it later in life, others can build it early in life.

The Lesson

Financial Discipline Is a Leadership Skill

Here's the truth every entrepreneur must face:

Your hustle can make you money, but your discipline will keep it.

Start with what you have:

- If you make $100, save $20.
- If you make $500, save $100.
- If you have inconsistent income, save a percentage, not a fixed amount.

Small savings grow. Consistency compounds. Discipline builds freedom. Building Your Financial Village

Success isn't just about money, it's about the people guiding and supporting you.

1. **Hire a knowledgeable accountant or CPA.**

   Not someone who just files taxes, but someone who helps you understand your financial life.

   Respect that relationship. If they've helped you grow, don't burn the bridge, communicate and collaborate.

2. **Work with a qualified financial advisor.**

   Ask questions. Demand transparency.

   A good advisor teaches you, not manipulates you.

3. **Build a strong internal team.**

   Your employees should feel valued, heard, and included.

   When your team feels connected to your mission, they protect your business with the same loyalty you expect from yourself.

A strong village, professionally and personally, is the backbone of long-term success.

Final Conclusion

Your Choices Shape Your Legacy

Tam's story, and the stories of many others, remind us that life doesn't always take a traditional path. Some of us find early success. Some of us build businesses out of survival. Some of us learn through trial and error.

The important part isn't how you start. It's how intentionally you prepare for where you're going.

In a society obsessed with fast money and instant rewards, financial planning becomes even more important. Behind every viral moment, big tip, or profitable month, there is a real life that needs structure, discipline, and vision.

This chapter isn't about judgment.

It's about preparation. It's permission to take control of your future.

To ask uncomfortable questions. To plan beyond your lifestyle.

To build wealth that lasts longer than your job title. Start with what you have.

Save as much as you can. Build a team that supports your growth.

Learn the financial tools that protect your future. And remember, you are not defined by how you make your money.

You are defined by:

- The decisions you make today
- The discipline you commit to
- The legacy you choose to build

Your beginning may not have been perfect, but your ending can be powerful.

Let this chapter be your blueprint. Let it be your warning. Let it be your motivation.

Because success is not just about how much you earn, it’s about how wisely you manage it, how responsibly you protect it, and what you leave behind for the next generation.

Your money has power. Your choices shape your future. And your discipline becomes your legacy.

Chapter 24
The Many Faces of the Entrepreneur

Starting a business is more than just creating a product or offering a service. It's a mirror. A mirror that reflects your habits, your fears, your strengths, and more importantly, your personality. As entrepreneurs, we don't just bring skills and ideas to the table, we bring ourselves. And sometimes, we are the very thing standing in the way of our own success.

Every entrepreneur walks into their business with a unique mindset, shaped by upbringing, past experiences, ego, fear, or ambition. Some of us are natural givers, others are takers. Some are strategic thinkers, while others act purely off emotion. Some are focused, and some are professional procrastinators. The truth is that there's no one-size-fits-all personality that makes a successful entrepreneur.

But there's one common thread among the most successful ones. They know themselves.

The Self-Aware Entrepreneur

Self-awareness is your superpower. The moment you understand who you are, not who you pretend to be for your brand, not who social media says you should be, but who you truly are at your core, is the moment you unlock the ability to grow. Knowing your strengths allows you to use them. Knowing your weaknesses gives you the power to improve or hire support. Ignoring them only delays your progress and caps your revenue potential.

Let's explore some of the personalities I've encountered over the years, in others and within myself.

1. **The Procrastinator**

This entrepreneur always has great ideas, but they rarely act on them. Their to-do list is long, but nothing gets crossed off. They wait for the perfect time to launch, file, respond, or take the next step. Unfortunately, perfect timing never comes.

The fix: Procrastinators need structure. Create deadlines. Break large tasks into small wins. Get accountability partners or coaches to keep you moving. Every day you wait, you lose potential income and growth.

2. **The Selfish Boss**

This personality only thinks about me. They want all the credit, all the profit, and none of the responsibility when things go wrong. They fail to see the power in building a team or empowering others.

The fix: Shift your mindset. Business is a team sport. Delegate, trust, and share the wins. Long-term success is built through collaboration, not isolation.

3. **The Over-Giver**

These are the entrepreneurs who give too much. They undercharge, over-deliver, and burn themselves out trying to please everyone. They confuse generosity with poor boundaries.

The fix: Understand your value. You can still be generous without sacrificing your profitability. Set clear pricing, boundaries, and learn to say no without guilt.

4. **The Taker**

The taker sees business as a one-way street. They want all the benefits, clients, referrals, and mentorship, but offer little in return. This mindset may work short-term, but it erodes trust and repels long-term growth.

The fix: Be intentional about reciprocity. Give value without expecting a return. Support others genuinely. Relationships matter in business, and givers go further.

5. **The Unaware Operator**

This business owner doesn't realize the energy they bring into a room. They're not aware of how they speak to staff, how they handle stress, or how their mood affects their brand. They often wonder why turnover is high or why sales are inconsistent, unaware that they might be the cause.

The fix: Start asking for honest feedback. Reflect on how you respond to pressure. Check your tone, presence, and leadership style. Emotional intelligence is just as valuable as business strategy.

6. **The Fearful Dreamer**

They have vision, but fear stops them at every turn. Fear of failure, fear of success, fear of rejection. They operate from a mindset of what if it doesn't work instead of what if it does.

The fix: Acknowledge the fear, but act anyway. Courage isn't the absence of fear; it's moving forward despite it. Surround yourself with bold people. Fear is contagious, but so is faith.

7. **The Control Freak**

   Everything must go their way. They won't delegate, won't trust their team, and often micromanage themselves into exhaustion. They confuse control with excellence.

   The fix: Learn to delegate with intention. Train people, document processes, and release your grip. Your growth is limited by how much you refuse to let go.

8. **The Visionary Without Execution**

   They play a big game. They have big plans, big dreams, and even bigger ideas, but never execute. They're always working on something, but rarely finish anything.

   The fix: Focus on finishing. Pick one thing. Launch it, test it, revise it, and complete it. Success is built on action, not talk.

The Power of Knowing Yourself

Here's the truth: we all have a mix of these traits. Some days we procrastinate. Other days, we lead with ego or fear. The key isn't to be perfect, it's to be aware.

When you know who you are, you can make better business decisions. You'll know:

- When you're self-sabotaging your own growth
- When your people-pleasing is eating your profit
- When you're controlling out of fear instead of leading with faith
- When your fear of being seen is holding back your brand

You can't fix what you won't face. That's why personal growth and business growth go hand in hand.

You don't just need a business plan; you need a mindset plan. One that checks your ego, your habits, and your emotions.

Final Thoughts

Business isn't only about marketing, sales, or systems. It's about people, and you are the first person your business depends on.

Know yourself. Audit your traits. Do the inner work.

Because the more you understand your personality, the more equipped you'll be to grow your business, expand your revenue streams, and build a legacy that lasts.

Your success begins with you. Own Who You Are, Then Grow from It

Every entrepreneur has dreams of success, but not every entrepreneur is willing to look in the mirror and confront what's really standing in their way.

You can have the best logo, the most talented team, and the flashiest marketing, but if your mindset, your habits, or your personality traits are flawed and unchecked, your business will always suffer.

You must know yourself. That's not a cliché, it's a requirement. Because the biggest battles in business aren't with competitors, they're internal. They show up in your procrastination, your pride, your fear of delegation, your inability to receive correction, or your refusal to charge what you're worth.

But here's the truth, you can't fix what you're not willing to face.

Your business will only grow to the level of your self-awareness.

Your revenue will only rise to the level of your responsibility.

Your legacy will only last as long as your willingness to evolve.

So stop blaming the market. Stop blaming your clients. Stop blaming your past. Start doing the real work internally. Because once you master yourself, your business becomes a tool for power, purpose, and profit.

This chapter is your call to action:

Audit who you are. Adjust where needed. And activate the version of you that your business truly deserves.

You don't just need a new strategy, you need a new level of self-leadership.

And once you unlock that, nothing and no one can stop your growth.

Chapter 25:
From Lessons to Legacy

If you've made it to this chapter, I want you to pause.

Not because the journey is over—but because what comes next requires honesty.

Everything you've read up to this point was intentional. Every story. Every mistake. Every collapse. Every comeback.

These were not fictional warnings or exaggerated case studies. They were real people, real businesses, and real consequences. In many of these stories, one decision—sometimes made in minutes—altered the course of an entire life.

And they were written for one purpose:
So you don't have to learn every lesson the hard way.

Throughout this book, you met entrepreneurs who were talented, driven, and willing to work themselves into the ground. People who had hustle, vision, and heart. Yet many of them still failed—not because they were lazy or unmotivated—but because they lacked structure, guidance, and sometimes the humility to ask for help.

Some trusted the wrong people.
Some ignored the numbers.
Some delayed change until delay became damage.

And the hardest truth of all?
Many of those outcomes were preventable.

Not because they were careless—but because they didn't know what they didn't know.

That is the most dangerous place an entrepreneur can be.

This book was never written to judge anyone. It was written to create awareness. Because you cannot fix what you refuse to see. And far too many business owners are building success on unstable foundations, believing effort alone will protect them.

It won't.

The Train That Tests You

Running a business is like being on a journey where you know exactly where you're going. You've mapped the route. You've calculated the time. You've promised clients, staff, and yourself that you'll arrive at a certain destination—on schedule.

Then suddenly, everything stops.

You pull up to a railroad crossing, and a train begins to pass. One container after another. Five minutes go by. Ten minutes. Cars stack up behind you. Some drivers get impatient and turn around, convinced there must be another way.

You consider it too.

But you already know this area. You've driven every road. You know the shortcuts. And every alternative leads to another dead end. So you stay.

Your patience starts to erode. Time feels wasted. Money feels lost. Your schedule is slipping, and frustration builds because this delay was never part of the plan. You get out of the car, hoping to see the end of the train—but all you see are endless containers rolling by.

There's no shortcut.
No driving through it.
No jumping over it.

So you wait.

Finally, relief—there's the end of the train. You rush back to your car. The gates lift. You put the car in drive.

Then the gates come back down.

Another train.

This one is shorter, but the frustration is heavier. Your patience is gone now. By the time you finally cross the tracks and reach your destination, something has shifted. The irritation you carried with you turns small problems into big ones. Your focus is gone. Your energy is drained.

And yet—as a business owner—you still have to perform.

You still have to lead.
Still have to make decisions.
Still have to show up confident and prepared.

Even when you're exhausted, irritated, and overwhelmed.

Now imagine doing that every single day.

That's entrepreneurship.

Delays. Setbacks. Interruptions. Unplanned obstacles.

The ones who survive aren't the ones who never face trains—they're the ones who learn how to wait without losing themselves.

Why Change Feels So Hard

As business owners, we build systems that work for us. They may not be perfect, but they're familiar. Familiar feels safe.

So when someone suggests a new way—an easier way, a more efficient way—we resist.

Not because it's wrong.
But because it feels like waiting for another train.

Change threatens control.
Change disrupts routines.
Change forces us to admit that what once worked may no longer be enough.

This resistance is strongest in those who have been in business five, ten, twenty years. Consistency kept them alive. Showing up worked. Hustling worked.

But here's the truth many avoid:

The world does not stop changing because you're comfortable.

Technology changes. Clients change. Regulations change. Expectations change. And when you refuse to adapt, clients don't announce their departure—they quietly leave.

Adaptation isn't optional.
It's survival.

When God Takes the Wheel

Someone once asked me why I accept change so quickly.

This is the story I shared.

Imagine God knocks on your door one morning and says, "Today, I'll drive you to work."

You're honored. Relieved. Excited. You get in the car, and He tells you to sit back and talk. Tell Him about your stress. Your worries. Your fears. He says, "I'll handle the drive."

As you talk, you notice He turns down a road you don't recognize. Then He gets on an expressway you've never taken. Your heart starts racing.

You've driven this route every day. You know the way. And this isn't it.

You check the clock. You're supposed to be at work in five minutes—and you're nowhere near your office.

You want to interrupt Him, but He keeps saying,
"Keep talking. Tell me what you need."

Finally, panic takes over.
"Where are you taking me? My job is in the other direction. I'm going to be late."

At that moment, He exits the freeway—and stops directly in front of your office.

Then He turns to you and asks,
"Can you explain how I got you here?"

You can't.

Because you were too busy believing you knew better. You forgot that He sees routes you don't. Shortcuts you've never noticed. Roads you didn't know existed.

All He asked you to do was trust Him.

The Legacy Question

This is how we live.
This is how we run businesses.

We grip the wheel because we've driven this road before—forgetting that someone else has been driving far longer.

There are countless books promising formulas, blueprints, and guaranteed success. And while many offer insight, none hold every answer—because every journey is different.

Even the people you admire once sat at the same train crossing. They didn't find *the* answer. They found *their* answer.

And here is the truth this book stands on:

No one has all the answers but God.

Business Fumbles was written to tell the truth—not polished success stories, but real ones. Stories that warn, prepare, and protect rather than impress.

Because truth helps.
Truth heals.
Truth protects legacy.

Final Conclusion: What This Book Was Really About

This book was never about mistakes.

It was about **what you do after you recognize them**.

It was about learning before loss, structure before collapse, and humility before consequences. It was about understanding that hustle without direction leads to burnout, and success without systems leads to ruin.

Every story in this book points to one truth:

Legacy is not built by effort alone.
It is built by awareness, structure, and willingness to change.

So before you turn the page, ask yourself:

- Where am I still holding the wheel out of fear, control, or pride?
- What warnings have I ignored because things "seemed fine"?
- What train am I refusing to wait for—at the cost of my future?

Because sometimes the most powerful move you can make as an entrepreneur

is not pushing harder—
it's letting go.

And in the next chapter, you'll see what happens when waiting is no longer an option—
when change shows up whether you're ready or not.

That moment is where businesses are either reborn
or quietly left behind.

Chapter 26: The Final Word — What You Do With What You've Learned

If you are reading this final chapter, you didn't just skim stories—you sat with them.

You walked through kitchens, offices, salons, warehouses, homes, courtrooms, and bank statements. You saw businesses rise on passion and collapse under pressure. You witnessed trust turn into liability, silence turn into loss, and success unravel because no one stopped to ask the hard questions soon enough.

This book was never meant to entertain you.
It was meant to **interrupt you**.

What All These Stories Had in Common

The people in *Business Fumbles* were not lazy.
They were not ignorant.
They were not incapable.

They were builders. Dreamers. Providers. Survivors.

Some were first-generation entrepreneurs.
Some inherited opportunity.
Some built from nothing.
Some had everything and still lost it.

What they shared was not failure—it was **exposure**.

- Exposure to trusting the wrong people
- Exposure to running businesses without structure
- Exposure to emotional decisions replacing professional ones
- Exposure to delaying hard conversations until consequences arrived
- Exposure to believing "it'll work itself out"

And here is the truth that runs through every chapter:

Most of the damage didn't come from bad intentions. It came from unprotected ones.

The Patterns You Were Meant to See

You saw what happens when:

- Family is given access without accountability
- Partners are trusted without agreements
- Cash flows without controls
- Titles are assumed instead of verified
- Taxes are minimized without thinking long-term
- Lifestyle is prioritized over sustainability
- Silence replaces oversight

You saw homes lost, businesses drained, health destroyed, and legacies threatened—not because people didn't care, but because they didn't protect what they cared about.

And you saw something else just as important:

Every collapse started quietly.

No alarms.
No dramatic warnings.
Just small decisions ignored over time.

This Book Was Never About Fear

It was about **responsibility**.

Responsibility to:

- Read before signing
- Ask before trusting
- Verify before delegating
- Separate love from leverage
- Put structure around success
- Plan for the future version of yourself

Fear paralyzes.
Responsibility empowers.

And empowerment is the real goal of this book.

What You Are Supposed to Take From This

If you take nothing else from *Business Fumbles*, take this:

1. **Hard work builds income. Structure builds longevity.**
2. **Trust is emotional. Protection is intentional.**
3. **Boundaries don't break relationships—lack of them breaks businesses.**
4. **Cash flow without control is not success—it's risk.**
5. **The goal is not to look successful. The goal is to stay successful.**

Every entrepreneur in this book wished they had paused sooner, asked better questions, or brought in help earlier.

You now have the advantage they didn't.

This Is Where Legacy Begins

Legacy is not what you post.
It's what survives you.

It's what remains standing when:

- You get tired
- You get sick
- The market shifts
- The people around you change
- Life interrupts your plans

Legacy is built when you decide that:

- Your business will not rely on luck
- Your finances will not rely on hope
- Your future will not rely on assumptions

Legacy requires uncomfortable conversations, professional guidance, and systems that work even when you're not there.

The Real Question This Book Leaves You With

This book does not end with answers.
It ends with responsibility.

Now that you know:

- What will you fix?
- What will you stop ignoring?

- What will you no longer excuse?
- Who needs to be removed from decisions they never earned?
- What systems need to be put in place—now, not later?

Because knowledge without action becomes regret.

Final Thought

Every story in this book proves one thing:

You don't lose everything at once.
You lose it decision by decision.

But the same is true for rebuilding.

Structure by structure.
Boundary by boundary.
Choice by choice.

Business Fumbles exists so that your story doesn't have to become another chapter.

Let this be the moment you stop fumbling—and start building something that lasts.

Acknowledgement

This book would not exist without the people who trusted me with their stories, their struggles, and their truth. To every entrepreneur who sat across from me with tears in their eyes, spreadsheets in their hands, and hope still in their hearts, this book is because of you. You allowed your failures, fumbles, and comebacks to become lessons that can now save someone else years of pain.

To my clients at Shewins Bookkeeping Services, thank you for trusting me not just as an accountant, but as a true partner in your growth. You have allowed me to walk beside you through IRS letters, payroll disasters, cash-flow crises, and major breakthroughs. Your journeys shaped every page of this book.

To my family and close friends, I am deeply grateful. Izabella Kolodka, thank you for your dedication, your help within my business, and for taking the time to listen, read, and support me as this book came to life. Shayonna Phillips, your marketing support, accountability, and constant reminders to keep pushing forward made a difference you may never fully realize. Your loyalty and belief in me will never go unnoticed.

To my daughter, Amber Smith, thank you for your hard work, for helping run the business, and for always keeping me grounded when I feel discouraged. You are a living reminder of what a strong mother-daughter relationship should look like. To my husband, thank you for loving me and standing in my corner through every meaningful project and every long night. Your support gives me strength.

To Michelle Bryant-Smith, thank you for always encouraging me and believing in my vision. And to my mother, Virginia Bryant, without your unwavering support I would not be where I am today. My love for you is deeper than words can express so I will simply say this: you are my rock.

To all my clients, friends, and family who supported me through long nights, missed calls, and the weight of carrying so many people's financial realities thank you for your patience, encouragement, and love. You reminded me that this work matters, even when it feels heavy.

And above all, I thank Jehovah God for the calling that led me here. Every client I met, every fumble I witnessed, and every lesson I learned was placed in my path for a reason. This book is not just a collection of stories it is an assignment.

Dedication

This book is dedicated to every entrepreneur who was never taught the rules of money but was expected to play the game anyway.

To the hustlers who built something from nothing.

To the dreamers who made money but didn't know how to keep it.

To the business owners who worked themselves to exhaustion still felt behind.

And to the women and men who were brave enough to start over when everything fell apart.

Business Fumbles is for you so that your next chapter is written with wisdom, structure, and the power to build a future that lasts.

About The Author
Sheila Williams, EA

Sheila Williams is the founder and CEO of Shewins Bookkeeping Services, Inc., a nationally respected accounting, tax, and advisory firm serving entrepreneurs across the United States. With more than three decades of experience in accounting, tax strategy, and financial recovery, Sheila has made it her mission to help Entrepreneurs turn confusion into clarity and chaos into control and avoid the costly mistakes no one warned them about.
As an Enrolled Agent (EA) licensed by the U.S. Department of the Treasury, Sheila represents clients before the IRS and specializes in helping entrepreneurs navigate audits, back taxes, payroll issues, and financial reconstruction. Her firm is widely known for stepping in when businesses are in trouble untangling years of mistakes, rebuilding financial systems, and putting companies back on track to profitability.

But Sheila's work goes far beyond numbers.

She has spent her career sitting across the table from business owners at their most vulnerable moments when partnerships collapse, when the IRS is knocking, when payroll is behind, when bank accounts are empty, and when fear replaces confidence. What she discovered is that most failures are not caused by a lack of hustle, talent, or ambition they are caused by missing knowledge, poor structure, and costly decisions no one warned them about.
Those real-life experiences led to the creation of Business Fumbles.

This book is built from real raw stories and hard lessons. As the host of the Business Fumbles Podcast, Sheila has sat down with business owners throughout her career who succeeded and fumbled...they unpack the decisions that cost them time, money, peace, and sometimes everything or barely survived because of financial blind spots and how they rebuilt. Every chapter reveals the truth that most business books avoid. Success without systems is fragile and most business failures are not caused by lack of effort, but by lack of education, structure, and the right guidance at the right time.

Sheila is also the author of

A Long Road to Success: Business Mistakes Are Preventable, and the creator and host of the Business Fumbles Podcast, where entrepreneurs share the mistakes behind their success, so others don't have to repeat them.

Known for her direct yet compassionate approach, Sheila bridges the gap between hustle and discipline, faith and finance, ambition and accountability. She is especially passionate about educating cash-based entrepreneurs, women in business, and first-generation business owners on how to protect what they build.

When she isn't advising clients, writing, or speaking, Sheila is focused on expanding financial literacy, mentoring entrepreneurs, and building legacy-driven businesses that last.

Business Fumbles is not just a book it is a warning, a guide, and a second chance for entrepreneurs willing to learn before the lesson becomes too expensive.

www.ingramcontent.com/pod-product-compliance
Lightning Source LLC
LaVergne TN
LVHW052246200926
848481LV00002B/291
* 9 7 9 8 2 9 5 6 8 4 0 3 6 *